John Pepper's ULSTER-ENGLISH DICTIONARY

John Pepper's
ULSTER-ENGLISH
DICTIONARY

Illustrated by
Rowel Friers

an Appletree haunbook

First published by
The Appletree Press Ltd
7 James Street South
Belfast BT2 8DL
1981

British Library Cataloguing in Publication Data
Pepper, John
John Pepper's Ulster-English dictionary.
1. English language—Dialects—Northern Ireland
—Dictionaries
I. Title
427'.9416'03   PE2587

ISBN 0-904651-88-6

Printed in Northern Ireland by Appletree Press Ltd

Foreword

If an Ulsterman is asked his opinion on a topic of the moment and replies that he has 'a nopen mine', he expects it to be appreciated that he has yet to come to a final decision on the issue. There are, however, many cases where he will not be instantly understood, and the aim of this guide to Ulster's 'morr tung' is to help clear the air for the bewildered.

Dictionary is another name for a word-book. This is such a work for it seeks to bring together many of those words which fall from the lips of Ulster people and yet are not to be found in a more conventional lexicon. It is impossible, for example, in a normal dictionary to look up such expressions as 'ironaf', the reply if you ask a Belfastman what he gets for his lunch, or 'nattalat', the answer you may receive if you inquire what someone is growing in his garden.

Colloquial speech is constantly changing. Words pass from regular use almost overnight and new ones are continually being added. Moreover, some of those listed in these pages may not be exclusive to Northern Ireland. Yet here is put on permanent record some elements of the unique word power which is a characteristic of the Ulsterman. It is not designed in any way as an academic work for the etymologist, but rather seeks to open the eyes of the man in the street to the consequences of opening his mouth, besides providing a helping hand to the visitor who is unaware that the advice 'nivver borr' means that the course of action he proposes is inadvisable, and who has never heard the word 'caheeing' applied to boisterous laughter.

abitchary, death notice, assessment of some deceased: 'They had a whole abitchary of him in the paper.' 'The abitchary said he had a wide circle of frens. A wonder where they come from?'

achanee, expression of regret, longing, disappointment: 'Achanee but my heart's broke so it is.' 'Achanee but the trouble comes thick and fast.' 'Achanee, my heart's scalded.'

acit, indication of finality: 'Acit as far as I'm concerned.' 'Acit, I told him. I'm not going till say anor word.'

ack, expression of frustration, impatience, annoyance: 'Ack I know the woman well, but I can't mine her name.' 'Ack I forgot to mine it.' 'Ack it's been a shackin day.'

ackay, statement of confirmation or agreement: 'Ackay, I got the job done ages ago.' 'Ackay, she's not a bad wee girl.'

afeard, timid, alarmed, scared: 'She's afeard of her own skin.' 'He always says he's afeard of nathin but don't you believe it.'

affis bap, descriptive of person whose mental capacity is in doubt: 'The fella's affis bap.' 'Everybody knew the referee was affis bap.' See **buckijit.**

aganny, extreme pain or distress: 'I'm in aganny with my chilblains.' 'The big pixture was a load of oul rubbitch. I was in aganny luckin at it.'

7

agatalaff, indicates that the speaker was highly amused: 'She's a rare turn. Agatalaff ivvery time I'm in her house.' 'He's a comedian, the same boy. Agatalaff when I meet him.'

agayon, once more, repetition: 'Do ahafta ast ye agayon.' 'Tell you what, Jimmy. I'll hev the same agayon.' 'I'm sick, sore and tired of him. He was rightly agayon last night. As full as the Boyne.'

ahafta, faced with no alternative: 'Ahafta go ni. It's late.' 'Ahafta speak till her about the way she's gettin on.' 'Ahafta make up my mine about it.'

a hinnae onny, indicates that stocks are sold out, that supplies are finished; 'A hinnae onny sex' in Ballymena means that the speaker's supply of potato sacks is exhausted: 'I'd lenn ye all the tay ye want onny a hannae onny.' 'Just nivver ignore her. She hannae onny sense.'

ahint, behind, immediately to the rear: 'She was stannin ahint him.' 'Keep ahint me, chile, or ye'll get yerself lost, and then where wud ye be?'

aleckadoo, club official, usually of a rugby club; committee member, often considered out of touch with reality, generally envied because he never has to pay for admission: 'Once the aleckadoos lay down the law there's nothing anybody can do.' 'The stand was full of aleckadoos.'

allabess, expression of friendship and goodwill on parting: 'Allabess, Jimmy. Seeya soon.' 'Cheerio fer ni. Allabess.'

amawayon, announces the completion of a visit, the resumption of a journey; to go home: 'Amawayon back to the house.' See **amferaff.**

amblence, specially-equipped vehicle for carrying patients to hospital: 'They tuck him away in the amblence.' 'I knew there was somethin up when I saw the amblence sittin at her dure.'

amferaff, announcement of impending departure: 'Nightall. Amferaff.' 'It's been a long day. Amferaff ni.' 'That was a great night. Great. Amferaff.'

8

amferbedni, indicates impending retirement for the night: 'Cheerio then. Amferbedni.' 'Amferbedni. Cud ye give me a glassa water in a cup? 'Amferbedni. Ahafta be up at the scrake av dawn.'

am gie fu, 1. indicates that the speaker's appetite has been fully satisfied: 'That was a right fry I got. Am gie fu and that's a fact.' 2. an admission of intoxication: 'Shee me? Am gie fu.'

ammastannininyerlite, seeks an assurance that the speaker is not obstructing another's view of a window display, procession, exhibition, etc: 'Ammastannininyerlite? If I am, I'll move over.'

amoany coddin, explains that the speaker doesn't want to be taken seriously: 'Don't go losin yir bap. Sure amoany coddin.' 'Ye know rightly amoany coddin. Can't ye take a joke?'

annahydion, ignorant, ill-informed person: 'I can't stand him. He's nathin but an annahydion.'

anol, all the extras, all that goes with a particular set of circumstances: 'He has a wee car anol.' 'They have a bungalow with a garden anol.' 'That wee girl has a fine leg anol.'

arcan, diminutive person or creature, midget: 'He was jumpin about like an arcan.'

Armay, refers to the speaker's daughter, May; can also refer to a sister or an aunt: 'Armay's a great wee dancer.' 'Armay's a quare wee scholar.' 'Armay gat three ayes anna no at her exams.'

arrwuns, members of our family, relations: 'Arrwuns is goin till Spain for wor holidays.' 'Arrwuns always go till Millisle.' 'Arrwuns wud give anything for a good fry.'

ashy pot, lover of the fireside, someone constantly cold: 'She's a desperate ashy pot. Always huggin the fire.' 'My oul woman's turned into a right ashy pot.'

assay, denotes that the hearer's attention is being sought, a call to listen: 'Assay there, wait till ye hear this.' 'Assay, Joe. Wud ye lissen to me a minnit?' 'Assay there. Wud ye catch yirself on?'

assee leff, inquiry seeking to establish if someone has gone home: 'Assee leff yit? It's about time he tuk hisself aff.' 'I've been luckin everywhere for him. Asse leff?'

9

ast, request, seek a favour, make an enquiry: 'Clare, t'migod he ast me to marry him.' 'I ast him a civil question but 1 didden get a civil answer.' 'All ye hev to do is to ast and ye know ye won't get it.'

aster, to make a request, to question a female: 'The onny way to fine out is to aster.' 'I aster point blank but she wudden open her bake.' 'Twice I aster and six times she said no.'

ate-the-bolts, describes someone who is a glutton for activity, a workaholic: 'That fella's a terrible ate-the-bolts.' 'See my oul woman? She fancies she married an ate-the-bolts. She huz anor think cummin.'

atterself, indicative of state of health: 'I knew the minnit she stepped across the dure she wasn't atterself.' 'That holiday did her a power of good. Ye cud see she's atterself again.'

aught, anything, nothing: 'I'm not well. I cannae dae aught in the house.' 'A cannae dae aught fer a hennae aught t'dae aught with.'

awa, indicates uncertainty, lapse of memory: 'I was talkin to awa last night. Y' know who I mean. The wee low set man with a stoop.' 'Did ye hear Awa on the television last night? Y' know? Thundergub.' 'I met Mrs Awa. She lives on the Ormo Road. The wumman that loves bakin tatey bread because it keeps her nails clean.'

awantin, sought for, needed urgently: 'Tell the wee girl she's awantin.' 'Me? Sure I'm always awantin. M'ma won't let me outav her sight.'

awayerthon, indicates disbelief, warns that the speaker is aware that his or her leg is being pulled; Ulster version of 'Tell that to the marines': 'Awayerthon, woman. I wasn't born yesterday.' 'Awayerthon, man, what d'ye take me fir?' 'Awayerthon, I'm not as green as I'm cabbage lookin, so I'm nat.'

awayon, 1. request to desist, to lay off: 'Awayon and take yirself aff. 'Awayon an claw moul on yirself.' 2. indication of departure: 'Am awayon ni. Goodnight.' 'Am awayon home.'

axit, door used for departure: 'I'm luckin for the axit out.' 'I cudden move for the axit was thick with people.'

 **bad scran,** bad luck, indicates disapproval: 'Bad scran to ye. Will ye get outa my road?'

bake, mouth, face: 'He always has his bake buried in the paper.' 'She toul me to shut my bake. I tole her she was pig iggerant.' 'When we're on our holidays I keep tellin him to hold his wee bake up till the sun.'

bakka beyond, remote, out-of-sight, distant: 'Sure their new house is at the bakka beyond.'

Ballet, abbreviation for 'William': 'Are Ballet's a bittava geg.' 'Ballet futted it the whole way without a murmur.'

Ballymena anthem, ironic Co Antrim description of 'What's in it for me?': 'Ast him to lenn ye a haun and you'll soon hear him at the Ballymena anthem.'

bap, bread roll: 'One toasted bap for his piece wud nivver satisfy our Alex. He hez t'hv thee.' 'After the wee girl got that bump on her head it was up like a bap.' 2. head: 'Don't lose yer bap over a wee thing like that. See **affis bap.**

barge, scold, abuse: 'She's only an oul barge.' 'Sure she barged the head aff me.'

barn, an exception: 'They all got samwitches barn me.' 'Everybody was there barn wee Sammy for he was sick.'

barney, 1. head, mind: 'Don't bother your barney.' 2. chat: 'We had a bit of a barney about old times.'

11

bat, blink, close one's eyes: 'A didnae bat an een all night.'

battle, bottle: 'D'ye want the sweeties outaffa battle or outaffa bax?' 'I'll have a battle by the neck.' 'I went to the chemist for a battle for my head and he ast me if I'd take it now. I said I'd wait till I got home and he gave me an awful funny look.'

baxer, pugilist: 'Geordie's a great wee baxer. Nivver gives in.' 'Are youngest says he wants to be a baxer when he grows up. He says he'll soon learn the ropes.'

beagle's gowl, denotes proximity, within hearing of the barking beagles during a hunt: 'I told him he wasn't within a beagle's gowl of the price I was lookin for the car.'

beara chews, footwear: 'I tole the man I wanted a beara chews for wearin.' 'See them beara chews? I bought them last week and they're lettin in already.' 'Them beara chews I got, the groun's started to come up through them.'

beelie, domestic cat: 'I caught my death of coul puttin the beelie out.'

beelin, suppurating, festering: 'The wee mite's heel was beelin.' 'I kept the wee lad from school for his finger was beelin.'

beezer, indicates excellence, approval: 'His drive from the first tee was a real beezer.' 'That goal was a beezer.'

bertie greetings, birthday good wishes: 'I gat bertie greetins on the radio.' 'Ye get sick listenin to them bertie greetins on the wireless.'

be-to-be, inevitable, unavoidable: 'Nathin you can do about it. Watter under the bridge. It be-to-be.'

bick, reverse, get back: 'Bick away there. Yer clear.' 'When a say "bick away" it means a want ye to bick away. Putter inta reverse.'

big, close, intimate, good friends: 'Him and her's got very big.' 'They've been big for a long time now, them two.'

binlid, stupid person: 'That fella's a binlid. I don't know what Minnie sees in him.' 'They were all binlids at the match last night.'

birl, dance expertly, nimbly: 'Armay can birl her leg.'

12

bisileek, bicycle: 'Alec's a great man for the bisileek.' 'I'm thinking of buyin him a pair of bisileek clips for his birthday.' 'I told the boss I was late because my bisileek started to kick up.'

bistick, biscuit: 'She gave me a cardboard tin of bisticks.' 'Ye used to be able to buy broken bisticks for next till nathin. Ni ye have to break them yerself and ye don't save a penny.'

bite, meal: 'I'm away down to my ma-in-law's for a bite.'

bittava, slight, sometimes used ironically: 'He's a bittava lad.' 'He's a bittava ijit.' 'He's a bittava geg.'

biz, is, act of being: 'If all biz well I'll be there.'

blackmouth, a Presbyterian, now little used.

blarge, crash into, behave roughly: 'She wasn't lookin where she was goin; that's why she blarged intil me.' 'I told him to take care or he'd blarge intil me.'

blether, garrulous person: 'Him, he'd blether the ears aff ye.' 'She's nathin but an oul blether. Nivver shuts up.'

blethercumskite, person who talks stupidly. See **blether.**

bley, dun coloured, pale and wan looking: 'Ye cud see she wasn't well. Her face was bley.'

bline-as-a-bat, indicates defective vision: 'The referee was as bline-as-a-bat.'

blinge, 1. drinking bout: 'He's been on the blinge for a whole week.' 2. hard blow: 'He gave him a right blinge. I wonder what came over him?'

blingle, bilingual: 'The wee girl's quaren good at the French. She's goin to be blingle.'

blink, unlucky person, apt to cast a shadow on proceedings: 'Don't ast him to come along. He's the blink.'

blirt, untrustworthy person, someone of poor character: 'The minnit I clapped eyes on him I knew he was a right blirt.' 'Onny a blirt wud act the way he behaved to my wee sister.'

boast, hollow: 'The Easter eggs I paid good money fer wuz all boast.'

boggin, untidy, unclean: 'The house was boggin so it was.' 'She's awful through-other. The place is always boggin.'

boke, vomit: 'The chile was bokin all night.' 'The way he kept chandering on and on nearly made me boke.'

bollox, muddle: 'You can bank on it. She'll make a bollox of the whole thing.' 'I spent hours explaining what it was all about but at the heels of the hunt she made a complete bollox of it.'

bookie, 1. bookmaker: 'Ye shud see the house my bookie's livin in. Onny for me he'd be livin in a hut.' 2. bunch of flowers: 'I cudden believe my eyes when he bought me a bookie for my birthday.'

booley, bandy: 'He's all booley-legged.'

borr, 1. borrow: 'I'd far rarr borr the farr's car.' 'I was onny in the house two mints when she was at the dure wantin to borr a quarter of tea.' 2. brother: 'His big borr takes the wee lad everywhere.' 3. bother: 'I told her to nivver borr her head.'

botch, carry out a task inefficiently, carelessly: 'He made a right botch of the job.' 'Ye wudden believe the botch he made of paprin the room.'

boul, 1. dish in which food is served: 'Nathin bates a good boul of parritch.' 2. cheeky, forward: 'She's a boul wee girl.' 3. lively person who is good company: 'The boul Harry was there as large as life.' 'It'll be all right once the boul Alex arrives.'

bout ye, greeting, an inquiry about your health; an indication of interest in your welfare; curiosity about your plans: 'How's bout ye?' 'Bout ye? An where d'ye think yer fir?' 'Bout ye, Jimmy. How's everything?'

boxty, dish consisting of grated potatoes, with flour and water added, then fried: 'A pan of boxty at night does a body a power of good.'

brattle, clap of thunder: 'I don't mine the lightnin. I can't stand the brattle of the thunder.'

14

brave, 1. more than just a few, considerable amount or distance: 'It's a brave wee bit down the road.' 2. indicative of a person of good character: 'She's a brave wee woman.' 3. descriptive of reasonable weather: 'It's a brave day.' 4. Not excessive: 'I'm feeling a brave bit better but I'm not right yet.'

bravely, 1. intoxicated but still in control, unlikely to survive a breath test: 'He was out for a fight for he was bravely.' 'I knew he was bravely when he ast me what I was hevvin.' 2. recovering from illness: 'After him being so bad he's doin bravely.'

braven offen, frequently, with regularity: 'She comes here braven offen.' 'Aye. I see him braven offen.'

braven worm, even temperature, tending to humidity: 'It's braven worm after the way it was yesterday.' 'It was braven worm this morning but its couler ni.'

breed, staff of life: 'The breed nowadays isn't what it was.' 'I always buy sliced breed. It saves ye cuttin it up.'

brew, employment exchange, unemployment benefit: 'My heart's broke trampin up and down to the brew.' 'Sure he spends more time at the brew than he does in his bed.' 'Goin aff the brew! That'll be the day.'

brock, leavings, suitable for pig feed: 'She was hingin on till his arm like a bucket of brock.'

bronical, victim of a bronchial condition: 'The oul lad's got terrible bronical trouble.' 'He's been bronical for years now.'

broughan, porridge: 'Nathin fills ye of a mornin than a bowl of hot broughan.'

brow, borrow: 'He wanted to brow our whitewash brush. He said he wanted to whitewash the yard wall blue.' See **borr.**

brunchle, a good handful, generous amount: 'I'll say this about Minnie. She'll always give ye a good brunchle.'

brung, brought, conveyed: 'He plays with the head, that boy. He brung her to the dance in his car.'

brusted, burst, punctured: 'Da, my balloon's brusted.'

buckijit, extreme type of idiot: 'That man's nathin but a buckijit.' 'I'm not goin to the match the day. The goalkeeper's nathin but a buckijit.' See **ijit** and **stupa ijit.**

bully, denotes approval, admiration: 'Bully Jimmy. How're ye feelin?'

bulk, flick with the fingers as in playing marbles: 'When I was a wee lad I wud bulk marleys all the time.'

bumsker, bomb scare: 'The traffic was held up because of a bumsker.' 'I'd a been here earlier onny there was an oul bumsker.'

bunnelascrap, worthless, used car: 'He tried to sell me a bunnelascrap. I ast him what did he take me for.'

bunse up, pool resources, go Dutch: 'I said I'd go with the others for a feed but only if we bunsed up.' 'We bunsed up and bought the scout-master a present.'

burr, butter: 'I always say ye can't bate country burr on yir bread.'

butterin up, flattering, cajoling: 'He's always butterin me up. Makes me sick.' 'He's a dab hand when it comes to butterin ye up.'

butt packet, pocket in a suit for small change or unfinished cigarettes: 'My butt packet's always full av butts.' 'Ye shud see my man's butt packet. It's like a midden.'

by the neck, used when ordering bottle of stout or beer, indicating that it should not be poured into a glass: 'Gawd but I have a thirst on me. A battle by the neck.'

cahee, laugh boisterously: 'They were caheein the whole night. The neighbours rapped on the wall.' 'Ye cud have heard the cahees of them a mile away.'

call, reason, excuse: 'There's no call for you to behave to me like that.' 'You've no call to spend all that money on rubbitch.'

callstanes, gall-bladder ailment: 'I nivver saw anything like her callstanes. If she brings them home she cud pebble dash the house with them.'

callus state, wake me at eight: 'Callus state for a hafta be at my work early.'

Car Door, a village in Co Down: 'Them two have lived in Car Door all their lives.' 'Quiet wee place Car Door, except when they have their motor bicycle race.'

carl singer, Christmastide vocalist: 'He's nivver in when its Christmas for he's a great wee carl singer.' 'When Christmas comes and they want a carl singer he's yer man. He just loves a cumallye.'

cast up, remember unkindly, accusingly: 'She cast up that oul jumper she gave me last year.' 'He's a divil and a half. He even cast up the trousers I didden give him for his birthday.'

catch yerself on, counsel of caution, warning against acting without considering the consequences: 'For God's sake use yer loaf. Catch yerself on, man.' 'I'll give ye the rounds of the kitchen if ye doan catch yerself on.'

cause girl, member of the chorus, professional dancer: 'She's onny a cause girl.' 'She's a grate kicker, a born cause girl.'

caution, 1. someone who is good company: 'She's a caution so she is. You should hear her.' 2. person to be wary of: 'Thon lad's worth watchin. He's a bit of a caution.'

champ, mashed potatoes, Ulster style: 'Shure nobody cud bate a good feed of champ.' 'That woman's champ fairly sticks to yir ribs.'

chander, bicker, quarrel, talk disagreeably: 'Chanderin's about the only thing that woman's any good at.' 'She's my sister-in-law and she's onny happy when she's chanderin.'

chaps, fried potatoes: 'Give him a plate of chaps an he's as happy as Larry.' 'My man just can't stand vinegar on his chaps. He goes for the salt, tho.'

cheesers, chestnuts, conkers: 'The wee lad loves playing cheesers.'

chegh, word used when herding a cow: 'The wee lad said he wanted to chegh the heifer intil the byre. He's a great wee help on the farm.'

cherry octopus, chiropodist: 'I wanted to go to the ospill to see the cherry octopus but I decided my fut cud hold on for anor week.' 'She's a great cherry octopus. Onny for her my feet wud hev left me.'

childer, offspring: 'Them childer wud drive ye astray so they wud.' 'The childer are a quare haunful.'

chile, infant: 'The wee chile's cryin her eyes out.' 'Just luck at her. The chile's a wee bunnel.'

chimley, chimney: 'That's the second time this week the chimley's went on fire.'

chokin, causing amusement: 'He tole me his shap was burgled and I said to him, "Yer chokin".' 'I was sure he was chokin when he said he'd won at the pools.'

clabber, wet, soft earth; mud: 'He was clabber up to the oxters.' 'There was clabber everywhere; it was shackin wire.'

clammy, uncomfortably hot, humid: 'It's an offal clammy oul day.' 'His hands were all clammy.'

18

clap, cow dung: 'I hate goin near that farm. I'm always walkin in cow clap.'

clart, untidy woman, through-other housewife: 'You should see that house of hers. She's nathin but a clart.'

clashbeg, tell-tale, person incapable of keeping a confidence: Ye cudden tell that one anythin. She's nathin but a clashbeg.'

clatter, 1. loud noise: 'She came a right clatter down the stairs.' 'You could hear the clatter he made a mile away.' 2. large quantity: 'She gave me a whole clatter of them.' 'I onny wanted two or three but I got a whole clatter.'

clatterbox, gossip, person incapable of keeping a secret, victim of a weakness for talking about other people's affairs: 'She's a born clatterbox.' 'She's that big a clatterbox you daren't tell her anything.'

clertma, emphatic declaration: 'Clertma goodness he tuk the light from my eyes when he drive me to the dance.'

clever, roomy, well-fitting, generously-cut garment: 'The coat she made me was that clever ye could camp out in it.' 'The suit was far too clever for him. He looked like a drowned rat.'

clinker, superbly good: 'That was a clinker of a shot you played.' See **clinkin**.

clinkin, first class: 'She's a clinkin wee dancer.' 'It was clinkin at the disco last night.' 'I had a clinkin time on my holidays.'

clipe, sizeable portion, considerable quantity: 'He has a right clipe of land.' 'I ast the grocer to give me a clipe of them ham bones.'

clockin, sitting, squatting: 'He sits clockin in front of the fire all day.' 'She sits at the winda like a clockin hen. She misses nathin.'

cloddin, throwing: 'They were cloddin petral bombs the whole night.' 'It's terrible the way they keep cloddin breeks at the police.'

clogher, cough violently and frequently: 'I'm goin to the chemist for something to stop my clogher.' 'He does nathin but sit there clogherin.' 'He has a clogher the like of which nobody ever hear before.'

clone, scent: 'I bought the missus a battle of clone to keep her quiet

clutey, left-handed, awkward: 'He can do nathin right. He's all clutey.' 'He's just like his da, clutey.'

cod, foolish individual, practical joker: 'He's onny an oul cod.' 'I tole him he was trying to make a cod outa me an I wudden stann it.'

cog, copy, imitate: 'Givvus a cog of your homework.'

coggley, unsteady, liable to collapse: 'This table's awful coggley.' 'When I wear them stillety heels it makes me feel awful coggley.'

cold fool, chicken served cold. 'Cold fool makes an awful nice bittava meal.'

collogue, converse intimately or in secret; a scheming exchange of confidences or gossip: 'The two of them is always colloguing.'

colour, small amount: 'Could I borrow a wee colour of milk.' 'I never take much milk in my tea. Just a wee colour.'

comestibles, food, provisions: 'I'll say this, she always has plenty of comestibles in the house.'

conservative, greenhouse: 'We have a wee conservative in the garden.' 'Harry gets great value outa the tomatoes he grows in the conservative.'

coorse Christian, rough diamond, person lacking in refinement: 'He's a coorse Christian if ivver there was one.'

corforus, request to be called for: 'Cud ye corforus atate?' 'He said he'd corforus and I know he'll keep his word. If he doesn't I'll show him the back of my haun.'

corned, cake or loaf baked with currants: 'I want a corned loaf.' 'Ye cudden bate a corned square.'

coul coort, indifferent, undemonstrative lover: 'He was a coul coort. I cud have kicked myself.'

coulter, sharp, cutting blade of a ploughshare: 'She has a nose like a coulter.'

cowboy, chancer, someone of dubious character: 'That fella's a right cowboy.' 'Thon was no football team. Nathin but a bunch of cowboys.'

cowerdy custert, person lacking in courage: 'Sure he's onny a wee cowardy custert.' 'When I raised my haun till him he tuk to his heels. A cowerdy custert.'

cowlrife, susceptible to the cold; shivery person: 'She's terrible cowlrife.' See **ashy pot.**

cowl swate, state of anxiety: 'I broke into a cowl swate when I saw the peelers.' 'We were both late for work and I was in a cowl swate when she said to me "Come on to hell Lizzie or the gates 'll be shut".'

cowp, overturn, upset: 'He cowped her intil the sheugh.'

crabbit, irascible, ill-tempered, carnaptious: 'He's that crabbit you wudden credit it.' 'She's as crabbit as the day and the marra.'

crack, lively, entertaining chat: 'Come on on in and givvus a bit of yer crack.' 'Jimmy's the quare crack.'

cratur, whiskey: 'It's hard to bate a wee drap of the cratur.' 'A wee mouthful of the cratur wud do ye no harm.'

creashy, dish for which dripping has been lavishly used: 'Thon supper was lovely an creashy.'

creepie, stool with three legs, steadier than the traditional four on an uneven cottage floor.

cribbin, kerb: 'I crigged my toe on the cribbin.' 'I was stannin on the cribbin waitin for somebody to take my arm across the road.'

croppen for all corn, someone expecting a meal, always hoping to be treated: 'Keep yer eyes skinned. She's croppen for all corn.' 'After buyin him two drinks I saw he was an oul croppen for all corn.'

cryin buckets, weeping bitterly: 'She was that upset she was cryin buckets.' 'She's awful touchy. He has onny to give her a cross look an she's cryin buckets.'

cumallye, folk song; musical house party: 'We'll have a bit of a cumallye to celebrate.' 'He sung his heart out at the cumallye last night. We were there till all hours.'

21

cut, 1. mortified, insulted, embarrassed: 'I was all cut after the things he said about me. He's very cuttin.' 'He tore intil her. She was all cut.' 'She cut me to the bone in Royal Avenue so she did.' 2. intoxicated: 'Ye cud see by the way he walked that he was half cut.'

cutty, little girl: 'She's a quiet wee cutty. Ye cudden help but tak till her.'

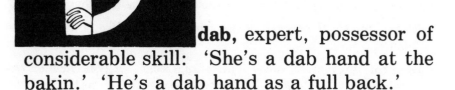 **dab,** expert, possessor of considerable skill: 'She's a dab hand at the bakin.' 'He's a dab hand as a full back.'

dacent spud, likeable character, reliable person: 'I'll say this about Joe, he's one dacent spud.' 'No matter what ye hev to say about her, I can tell ye her man's a dacent spud.'

dander, 1. leisurely stroll: 'John's just gone out for a wee bit of a dander.' 2. temper: 'She always gets my dander up. She's a terrible woman.'

dawdle, short distance, simple task: 'Sure it was only a wee dawdle down the road.' 'That job was just a dawdle.'

day dawn, exactly in position: 'Them two enns of the pipe hev to be day dawn.'

dayligone, twilight, dusk: 'I love just sitting at dayligone thinkin long.'

day mare, popular daily newspaper: 'I always buy the "Day Mare". I like its palitics.' 'The only two papers we read is the "Day Mare" an the "Partial Reporter".'

dead enn, amused, astonished: 'He was a quare geg so he was. I tuk my dead enn at him.'

deadly crack, tremendous fun: 'We had a great night. It was deadly crack.' 'I wudden hev missed that wake. It was deadly crack from the word go.'

23

dear, expression of despair or deep feeling: 'Dear knows what has come over the wee girl.' 'Dear a dear but I feel awful. My head's turned.'

deed, deceased: 'His wife's deed this twelve month.' 'Her husband's deed an gone.' 'That fella's deed from the neck up.'

deeve, to deafen, annoy: 'The wireless was that loud it wud deeve ye.' 'It wasn't much of a party. I was just deeved the way they behaved.'

denise, niece: 'I brought denise with me.' 'Denise is a great wee dancer.'

detergent, preventive, cause of discouragement: 'A policeman on the beat is a great detergent.' 'The best detergent is a peeler roun the corner.'

dialect, abandoned, deserted: 'They're all dialect houses in that street.' 'I tole the rent collector he hadda nerve astin me to pay just to live in a dialect house.'

diclas, absurd, preposterous: 'Doan be diclas. You're talkin rubbitch.' 'Absolutely diclas. It's a latta nonsense.'

dig, violent blow: 'I'll give you a dig in the bake if you aren't careful.' 'When I gave him a dig it brought him to his senses.'

dinge, damage, dent: 'You can see the dinge where he hut my car at the corner.' 'I got a dinged tin of peas and I'm not goin to pay for them.'

dinger, indicates speed, rapidity of action: 'When I saw him he was goin a right dinger.' 'I knew he'd hit something. He was goin a dinger when he went roun the corner.'

dinnel, throbbing or tingling pain: 'I have a dinnel in my hinch.'

dinnelin, trembling, state of a child's hand on a bitingly cold day: 'It was gie coul. The wee girl's hauns were dinnelin.'

dip, fried bread: 'My man's dyin about dip.' 'Sure ye cudden bate dip bread. That's what I always say.'

dipt soda, fried soda bread: 'Dipt soda with an egg, sure ye couldn't bate it.' 'Give him two or three pieces of dipt soda and there's nathin he wudden do for you.'

24

dirt bird, contemptible, unreliable individual: 'She's a dirt bird an he's not far behine her.' 'Sure the whole fambly's nathin but a lock of dirt birds.' 'I wudden be beholden to a dirt bird like him.'

diseased, passed away: 'I knew the diseased woman terrible well. It was a lovely funeral.' 'The diseased man said if he was spared he wanted to be buried in Carmoney.'

dishabells, underclothes: 'She came to the dure in her dishabells. I didden know wherta luck.'

divid, separated, split into separate portions: 'The three of us divid the orange up, fifty fifty.' 'I always say, the world's ill divid.'

dobbin, school truancy, absenteeism: 'He was dobbin school again yesterday, the wee ruffian.'

doina line, showing affection, paying court: 'That fella's been doina line with are Minnie since Christmas.'

Doke, Doagh, village in Co Antrim: 'He comes from near Doke.'

dollop, large portion, generous helping: 'She gave me a right dollop of her stew.' 'Givvus a dollop of that champ there. I'm starvin.'

donkeys, long period of time (abbrev. of 'donkey's years'): 'I've been waiting at this bus stap for donkeys.' 'Sure my man's been breedin grewhouns fer donkeys.'

donsey, cuddly: 'She's a right donsey wee girl.'

dorient, chemical preparation to remove body odours: 'I bought him a battle av dorient for farr's day and he was all cut.' 'When the wire's hat a body needs their dorient.'

dornlaw, wife of the speaker's son: 'I ast the dornlaw up for a bite.' 'The dornlaw's very obligin.' 'The dornlaw's a right cook.'

downteel, shabby, poorly dressed: 'Ack ye cudden help feelin sorry for him. He's all downteel.'

dozer, lazy person, someone careless in behaviour and appearance: 'That fella's no dozer.' 'Keep yer eyes skinned. She's no dozer when it comes to Number One.'

drap dead, a Belfast retort: 'He said he was tryin to help and I tole him to drap dead.' 'The man ast me how he cud get to the cemetery and I tole him, drap dead.'

drapton, surprised, astonished, taken aback: 'She was fairly drapton when he walked intil the room.' 'I was drapton all right when she handed me back the poun she borrowed.'

draw, prepare a pot of tea: 'You nivver giv that tay time to draw.' 'Let the tay draw for a wee while. It's good for it.'

dree yer weird, be patient, hold your horses: 'Take yer time, man. Dree yer weird there.'

dreuth, alcoholic: 'Him? Sure he'd drink it outaffa bucket. A right dreuth.'

drib, small amount: 'I onny want a wee drib of sugar. Just as much as you'd hardly see.'

dribble, 1. small amount: 'I think I'll make a wee dribble of tay.' 'I nivver take much milk in my cup. Just a wee dribble.' 2. expert footwork during a soccer game: 'Alec was able to dribble it through the whole team. Alec's outa this world on the feel.'

drinka water, person of little account, someone considered a pain in the neck: 'He's like a long drinka water.' 'She sat there like a long drinka water.'

drippin, wet, soaked to the skin: 'It was that warm the sweat was drippin aff me.' 'He walked intil the house drippin.' 'I got caught in that shire and I'm drippin.'

drookit, wet through, soaked by rain: 'The water was pourin aff me. I was drookit.' 'Spoarin and I'm drookit.'

dropsies, game played with cigarette cards, the aim being to drop a card from a distance so that it touches or covers one already on the ground: 'When I was a wee lad we had great fun playin dropsies.' 'Member the time we played dropsies from your windey sill? Them wus the days.'

dry nod, disapproving indication of recognition: 'I just gave her a dry nod. I nivver liked the woman.'

ducle, cockerel with no fighting instincts: 'Don't bother yer head puttin money on thon ducle. You'll only lose it.'

dug, carnivorous domestic pet: 'That's a nice wee dug. Does he bark?' 'I hadda get rid of ar wee dug. He wudden give the postman peace.'

dummy tit, baby comforter: 'Give the chile her dummy tit or she'll roar the house down.' 'He lost the chile's dummy tit on me an we didden get a minnit's peace the whole night long.'

dun, tired out, exhausted: 'I've been at it since I got up an I'm dun.' 'To tell ye the truth I'm dun out. I want to get my feet up.'

duncher, cloth cap: 'It was a big funeral. There wussent a duncher to be seen.'

dunder, loud noise: 'Give her dure a dunder or she'll nivver hear ye.'

dundint, superfluous employee: 'Ever since he was made dundint he doesn't know what to do with himself.' 'It broke his heart when they told him he was dundint.'

dunt, blow: 'He hut me a quare dunt.' 'I got a dunt at the back an I onny had the car a fortnight.' 'I was stannin there mindin my own business when I gat this dunt.'

dunty, awkward, carnaptious person, unsatisfactory husband: 'He's a right oul dunty. Nivver borr yer head about him.' 'The truth is I married a dunty, Gawd help me.'

durbly, feeble, infirm: 'The aunt's got awful durbly on her feet.'

dure knacker crepe, black ribbon material used to indicate death in the house: 'She said she was goin till the shap to buy some dure knacker crape and I knew then he'd kicked the bucket.'

dynamite, jewellery: 'She lucked lovely. She was wearin dynamite earrings on her ears.'

eddick, pain, problem causing anxiety: 'Don't talk to me. I've gotta splittin eddick.' 'That fella gives me a eddick.' 'I only wish you had my eddick or you wudden be grinnin all over yer face.' 'Them rheumatic drills are an awful eddick.'

een, organ of sight: 'I didnae bat an een the whole night.' 'He's had his een on that wee girl this good while.'

Eggy, family abbrev. for 'Agnes': 'I always say Eggy has nice herr.' 'Eggy takes after me.' 'Wee Eggy has my head turned.'

ekker, school homework: 'The wee fella was sittin up till all hours doin his ekker.' 'His da's useless when it comes to givin the chile a haun with his ekker.' 'The poor wee fella can't get his ekker done with the tally blarin away there.'

enn, finish, death: 'I was foundered last night. I near got my enn.' 'One of these days he's goin to be the enn of me.' 2. extreme in amusement: 'He was quare fun. I tuk my enn at him.'

ern, journey with a specific purpose: 'Wud ye go a wee ern for me?'

esset, inquiry concerning the price of an article: 'I ast him how much esset an he give me a luck.' 'Esset dear? If it is I'm not going to borr my head.'

Extortion, type of flower: 'I'm away down till the shap to buy a packet of Extortion seed.' 'The wumman next dure always has a great show of Extortions.'

28

failed, in poor health, ailing: 'He looks quaren failed.' 'I tole him he needed a holiday for he was awful failed lookin.'

fairly, superlatively, excellently: 'The wee lad can fairly run.' 'She fairly tole him aff.' 'She fairly went for him.'

fairy eyes, conspicuous, prominent: 'He did it before my fairy eyes.' 'I watched her with my fairy eyes.'

falorey, lovable, mischievious person; implies harmlessness: 'He's the wee falorey man.'

fancy woman, mistress: 'Everybody knows she's been his fancy woman for years.'

farn, alien, not of British manufacture: 'They were all drivin farn cars.' 'Sure ivverybody's drivin a farn car these days.'

farr, a male parent, breadwinner: 'I'd far rarr borr the farr's car.' 'He's been a good farr to the childer.'

farry, roof-space in which to store guns and sharp tools out of reach of the children; otherwise faraway: 'Sure ye'd be in quare street without yir farry.'

fash, fish: 'I always get my fash from a man goin roun.'

Father Chart, imaginary deceased cleric: 'Our Father Chart in heaven.'

feel, venue for parade or demonstration: 'I always go to the feel on the Twelfth.'

feminate, not masculine: 'He had a feminate accent.'

fer, intended destination: 'Wherrer ye fer?' 'Are ye fer bed?'

fernenst, in front of: 'I can see her. She's stannin fernenst the pillar box.' 'Ye couldn't miss it. It's fernenst the Post Office.'

fernuf, acceptable, reasonable: 'What you're sayin is fernuf.' 'Fernuf, Harry. I'm game.'

ferr day, regular gathering for sale of goods or farm stock: 'It was the ferr day an everybody was there.' 'Everybody gets full on the ferr day.'

ferrdoos, shared equably: 'It was ferrdoos all roun. It's the only way.' 'Ferrdoos. I'm happy.'

ferr piece, substantial distance: 'Ye'd better get yir skates on for it's a ferr piece down the road.' 'It's a ferr piece to that new house of theirs.'

fice, front part of the head: 'He always has a fice on him that would turn a funeral.' 'Know this, that woman's fice wud scare a goat aff its tether.'

figure, attire for warm day: 'I saw her out in her figure yesterday.' 'It's far too coul to go out in yer figure.'

finaglin, dodging, scrounging: 'He's a fly man. He'd finagle his way outava strait-jacket.' 'If finaglin will get it for him he's yer boy.'

fissick, pick-me-up: 'I ast the dacter for a wee fissick for my stummick.'

fisslin, rustling noise: 'I cudden hear a word of the sermon for the fisslin in the pew behine us.'

flaffin, waving about: 'Wud ye tell yer wee girl to stap flaffin her lally?'

flannin, face cloth: 'I don't know what kine of a fambily I hev. I can nivver fine the flannin.' 'There son. Give yer wee face a rub with the flannin.' 'There's a flannin in the jawbox if ye want to wash yer face.'

flire, 1. flour: 'Them spuds is like balls of flire.' 'My favourite flire is oatmeal.' 2. flower: 'He had a wee flire in his buttonhole.'

flooter-futted, awkward, unskilled, esp. footballer: 'That fella's a dead loss. With a wide open goal in front of him he stans there, flooter-futted.' 'That right back's that flooter-futted he cudden even lace his boots.'

flure, floor: 'She scrubs her guts out keeping that flure spotless.'

fly man, untrustworthy person, someone to watch warily: 'Keep yer eye on that fella. He's a fly man.'

foam, telephone: 'Them foam stamps is quaren handy for futtin the bill.' 'Once she gets on the foam she'd talk yir head aff.' 'I foamed him up three times runnin.'

foe, the number above three: 'I always like a cuppa tea about foe.' 'The foe of them landed in on me outa the blue.'

fog feed, lavish meal: 'She gave him a whole fog feed.'

fonly, conditionally: 'Fonly a hadda knew about it a wudda went.' 'Fonly ye'd toul me at the time I wudden have opened my mouth.'

footer, fumbler, one who acts awkwardly: 'He's nathin but a footer.' 'He wasted the whole night footerin with a screw driver.'

forby, as well as, in addition to: 'I'll have a quarter stone of potatoes and some scallions forby.' 'Givvus a pint of milk and half a dozen eggs forby.'

foundered, chilled, suffering from exposure: 'I was foundered so I was.' 'What a night that is. I'm foundered.'

fren, companion, person with whom one is on good terms, close acquaintance: 'I've been a fren of his for years.' 'He isn't a fren. I only know him.'

fronted, insulted, mortified: 'She fronted me before the whole fambly.' 'I was nivver so fronted in my whole life.' 'I tole her I wassent there to be fronted.'

full, intoxicated, merry: 'That fella gets full at the least excuse.' 'He cudden see where he was goin for he was full to the gills.'

fummel, to fumble. See **footer**.

funky knuckles, awkward person, player who fails to use proper technique during a game of marbles: 'Him? Sure he's onny an oul funky knuckles. Useless.'

futless, intoxicated, incapable of walking steadily: 'He came home futless two nights runnin.'

futted, walked, travelled on foot: 'Last Twelfth I futted it every fut of the way.'

futtinit, going on a journey by foot: 'I know it's wet but I'm futtinit.' See **futted**.

 **gab,** talk, chatter: 'That woman's all gab.'

galeeried, bird-brained, incapable of serious thought: 'Don't expect a word you'd understand from a galeeried character like him.'

galluses, braces: 'Don't forget yer galluses or you'll make an exhibition of yourself.'

gan, gone, going: 'She's gan hame.'

gansey, woollen jersey, sweater: 'I was sitting there a whole hour before I found my gansey had crept up on me.'

gantin, yawning: 'I tole him I was sick watching him gantin in front of the bax all night and he should get to his bed.'

gaunch, ignoramus, someone who behaves badly: 'Ye can expect nathin from a gaunch like him but bad manners.'

gebbin, talking, gossiping: 'She was stannin at the dure gebbin her head aff.' 'She nivver staps gebbin. Ye'd think the wumman was woun up.'

geek, peep, look cautiously or secretively: 'Take a wee geek and see if she's cummin.' 'I was just takin a wee geek down the street.'

geelug, earwig: 'I always give the pillow a good shake before I get intil bed. I'm dead scared of geelugs.'

geesalite, request for a light: 'Mister, cud ye geesalite?'

geg, 1. mock, poke fun at: 'She was geggin me.' 2. amusing person: 'He's a quare geg. I nearly did myself an injury laughing at him.'

33

getstuckin, start working without delay: 'You'd better getstuckin before it gets dark.' 'I told him to getstuckin or we'd never get to our beds.'

gettinmairdun, obtaining the services of a hairdresser: 'My feet's got that sore poundin roun the shops I've made up my mine. I'm gettinmairdun.'

giffover, desist: 'I wish ye'd giffover so's we can get a bitta peace.' 'I tole him to giffover but he wudden lissen.'

girn, complain, grumble incessantly: 'She's just an oul girn.'

girney gub, constantly crying child: 'Her wee lad's only a girney gub. Ye cudden satisfy the wee brat.'

gitaffye, instruction to get undressed: 'It's time to gitaffye.' 'Wud ye go and getaffye? It's after yer bedtime.'

gitonye, instruction to get dressed: 'Wud ye go and getonye? We're late.'

givverit, make it available to her: 'When yer da says givverit then givverit.' 'Givverit and stap teasin the wee girl.'

givvitadunt, hit: 'See our television? I always find if ye givvitadunt it starts.' 'That's his door. Givvitadunt there and he'll know it's us.'

givvusabit, request for a small portion: 'Givvusabit of yir orange.'

givvushare, see **givvusabit.**

glar, thick, sticky mud: 'My shoes is ruined. The road was all glar.'

gleed, 1. low light: 'You cudden see in front of you. She had hardly a gleed about the place.' 2. possessions: 'He went through his money like water. The man hasn't a gleed. Sure, his da drunk a ten acre farm. Didden ye know?'

gleek, peep: 'Take a wee gleek through the winda.'

glype, stupid, thick-headed person: 'I always said he was a born glype.' 'That fella's a glype of the worst water.'

goin strong, keeping company: 'They've been goin strong this good while.' 'That wee girl's gatta quare hoult of him. They've been goin strong for months.'

gommeril, fool, stupid person: 'He's a gommeril and that puts it in a nutshell.'

good mine, intention, resolve: 'I've a good mine to write to the paper about it.' 'I've a good mine to go and see the man face to face.'

goosegab, gooseberry: 'Sammy's mad about goosegab jam.' 'Goosegab pie's hard to bate, I always say.'

gorb, person who overeats or shows greed: 'Minnie's a greedy wee gorb.' 'Gorb? Sure she'd ate ye outa house and home.'

gorbitch, inedible food, meal not easily digested: 'She's give me a loada gorbitch for my dinner.'

gormless, silly, lacking in wit: 'The man's gormless.' See **buckijit**.

got away, died, esp. after a long illness: 'John got away last night.'

gowlin, crying, whinging: 'Her wee chile's always gowlin.' 'Give the cradle a bittava rack. Maybe that'll stop the gowlin.'

gowpen, handful, as much as can be held in the hand: 'Cud ye lenn us a gowpen of male?'

great, 1. on friendly terms: 'They fell out but himinhur's great again.' 2. considerable: 'The picture was great. I cried my eyes out.' 'Thon wee comedian was great.'

greet, cry, weep: 'What d'ye want to greet for? That won't bring the poor man's leg back.' 'Her ma was greetin all through the weddin. You'd have thought it was a wake.'

griddle, cooking utensil, used particularly for baking soda bread: 'When she has the griddle on the smell of thon soda bread wud melt a heart of stone.'

gub, mouth: 'Wud ye shut yer gub?' 'He hut me a blow on the gub.'

guess, used for cooking; type of cooker: 'I'd farr rarr have guess than the lektrick.' 'One thing about our guess cooker you can nivver guess what the bill will be iike.'

guff, cheek, impertinence: 'Don't give me any of yer oul guff. I won't take it from you.'

gulder, shout, call out loudly: 'She let out a gulder at me.'

gully, breadknife: 'Sliced bread's all right but give me my oul gully every time.'

gulpin, brainless person, lacking in intelligence: 'The minnit I set eyes on him I knew he was a gulpin.'

gumboil, swelling on the cheek: 'She asked the chemist could he give her something for a gumboil in her hinch.'

gunk, disappointment, failure to reach expectations: 'He got a quare gunk when I didn't turn up.' 'When he heard I wasn't going to have anything to do with him he got a bit of a gunk.'

gunterpake, silly person, fool: 'What else wud ye expect from a gunterpake but stupidity?'

guttery, muddy: 'The streets is all guttery. My stackins is all japped.'

gutties, plimsolls, gym shoes: 'He's away for a run roun the corner in his gutties. The man has no sense.'

gyanbad, seriously ill: 'He's gyanbad. Even when the dog went into the room it kep its tail between its legs.'

gye, considerable: 'This parcel's gye and heavy.'

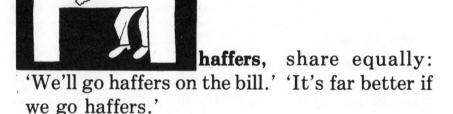**haffers,** share equally: 'We'll go haffers on the bill.' 'It's far better if we go haffers.'

haffun, standard spirit measure: 'We'll sit down over a haffun an see how we stann.' 'Sure a wee haffun nivver done anybody a bit of harm.'

half ture, intoxicated but not quite drunk: 'Listenin to the way he was talkin ye could tell he was half ture.'

hallion, irresponsible person, good for nothing: 'They were runnin roun like a crowd of hallions.'

happed up, wrapped up cosily, tucked in: 'Is the baby happed up?' 'The wee lad's happed up fer the night. Now I can get my feet up.'

hard chaw, rough, uncouth character: 'Thon fella doesn't know the meanin of a civil answer. He's a right hard chaw.' 'I cudden truss that boy an inch. He's a hard chaw if ivver there was one.'

harp six, turn upside down, up-end: 'I went harp six on the frosty road.' 'Sammy tripped and went harp six. You should have seen him.'

harra fillum, frightening movie: 'We saw a great harra film last night. I didden sleep a wink.' 'It's hard to bate a good harra film. If only Harry wudden go to sleep.'

harrished, tormented, harassed: 'I've been harrished the whole morning.'

hartacorn, describes generosity, warmth, forgiveness: 'There's nathin Maggie wudden do for ye. She has a real hartacorn.' 'Jimmy has a hartacorn. Sure he'd give ye the sleeves outa his waistcoat so he wud.'

hate, 1. anything: 'I don't know a hate about it.' 2. warmth: 'I cudden get any hate intil my bones. It was freezin.'

haun, hand: 'He took a right haun outa me.' 'I'll give you a bitava haun if you like.' 'Lennus a haun and don't just stann there, yer two arms the one length.'

haunless, awkward, ham-fisted: 'The man's just haunless with his feet.' 'Oul Jimmy's a haunless glype.'

hayeawlwiye, inquiry to establish if one has everything prepared for a departure: 'Are you sure ni? Hayeawlwiye? You've left nathin?'

headbin, dolt, dunderhead: 'He's nathin but a headbin.' 'I know you'll call me a headbin but I know Linfield will bate them intil the groun.'

head bomadeer, head waiter, foreman, overseer: 'Get me the head bomadeer. This stake isn't fit for a dog.' 'Hurry up, Jimmy, or the head bomadeer'll go fer ye.'

head-the-ball, unpredictable person, someone liable to make stupid decisions: 'Don't listen to a word he says. He nathin but a head-the-ball.'

heart scalded, bothered, troubled, harassed: 'That wee girl has my heart scalded.'

heavy metal, exclamation indicating astonishment, warning of impending disaster: 'Heavy metal! You don't say.' 'Heavy metal! Wud ye watch where yer goin.'

heesawun, a character, one who draws attention to himself: 'Heesawun. He always was a bit of a boyo.'

heff iate, eight-thirty (esp. in Ballymena): 'I'll be along about heff iate.'

he hadda view, intoxicated: 'Ye cud tell he hadda view. He was talkin funny.' 'Anybody cud see he hadda view. I wud hev said he was stovin.' 'He hadda view all right for as far as I cud see the man was futless.'

hellferlire, going at full speed, in a hurry: 'I saw him going hellferlire down the road.' 'The fella flew past me, hellferlire.'

hennae, denies possession: 'A hennae onny.' 'He says I hennae an ounce of sense. Imagine sayin a thing like that!'

hepney, coin which vanished with metrication: 'When I was a wee lad I used to buy a hepney worth of liquorice allsorts. They were lovely.'

herr, growth on the head: 'She has awful nice herr.' 'I'm away to get my herr done.'

heswainthead, someone who has lost his senses: 'Don't heed him. Sure heswainthead.'

hice, house, home: 'We have an awful nice we hice ni.' 'She lives in a funny hice. The front door's at the back.'

hiltnirhare, evidence of existence or presence: 'I saw nire hiltnirhare of them.' 'I looked high and low but there wasn't hiltnirhare of them.'

himinhur, married couple, sweethearts: 'Himinhur's been married over a year now.' 'Himinhur ast us down for a drink.' 'Himinhur make a right pair.'

himself, 1. husband, head of the house: 'Is it himself you want? He's weedin in the garden.' 'I'll have to have a word with himself about it.' 2. employer, boss: 'I want to see himself to see if he'll let me have the day aff.' 3. outstanding personality: 'It's himself coming on to the platform now. Isn't it great?'

hinch, upper part of the human leg, thigh: 'I tole the dacter I had a pain on my hinch.'

hirple, limp, walk with difficulty: 'He can hardly hirple down the road.' 'I watched him hirple past the dure this morning. I gotta laff.'

hiyew, exclamation demanding attention: 'Hiyew, who do you think you are?' 'Hiyew. Am I right for Chadally Street?'

hoke, scoop out: 'Wait a minute till I hoke out the fire.'

hough, breathe heavily, expel warm breath: 'Wud ye hough on the winda? It's all steamed up.'

howl awn, advice to take your time, not to be too hasty: 'Howl awn there till we see what's what.' 'Wud ye howl awn for a minnit? There's no desprit hurry.'

huffs, thighs: 'Didye see her skirt? It was away up till her huffs.'

hug-me-tight, shawl that can be fastened, woollen vest: 'It was that coul she wore her hug-me-tight in bed.'

huir inna Honda, careless driver of a foreign car: 'I was giv a dunt by a huir inna Honda and I onny had the car a week.' 'A huir in a Honda backed intil me and nivver had the dacency to stap. Make ye spit.'

hunkers, heels: 'He was sittin there onnis hunkers.' 'She was down on her hunkers in front of the fire.'

hurstle, hoarseness: 'I have a wee bittava hurstle.'

hurwuns, wife's relations: 'When hurwuns come ye can't hear yir ears. Everyone of them has talk for two rowsa teeth.' 'Hurwuns wud ate ye outa house an home.'

hut, hit, deliver a sharp blow: 'He hut me in the face so he did.' 'I didn't open my mouth but he hut me in the eye.'

 **iggerant,** uneducated: 'He's as iggerant as sin.'

ijit, idiot, stupid person: 'He's an oul ijit and I tole him so till his face.' See **buckijit.**

incentative, an encouragement to action or effort: 'There's no incentative to do a day's work nowadays.'

intended, fiancée: 'I suppose you and your intended will be at the dance?'

ires, long period of time: 'He clocks in front of the fire for ires on enn.' 'I was waiting for him for ires. I fairly lit intil him.'

irn, smoothing iron: 'I always irn of a Friday.' 'I'll have to go in and irn.'

ironaf, fixed period of time: 'I always get an ironaf for my lunch.' 'I've been stannin her waitin fer ye for a good ironaf.'

italiation, revenge for an insult or injury: 'I hut him in italiation.' 'They wudden let him intil the house and he set it on fire in italiation.'

jacked duncher, cloth cap with checked pattern: 'He was all dressed up in his jacked duncher.' 'He was at the match on Sardy. I saw his jacked duncher.'

jamember, request to recollect: 'Jamember the day we went to Bangor and you nearly cowped the wee boat?' 'Jamember when ye cud get to Bangor and back for a bob?'

japped, muddied: 'The road was that guttery after the rain that I got my tights all japped.' 'Them japs is terrible hard on yer nylons.'

jar, drink (esp. alcoholic): 'Ye'll have a wee jar afore ye go.' 'We've time for a jar, haven't we?'

jawbox, kitchen sink: 'Put the dishes in the jawbox, wud ye?' 'Me? Sure I spend half my life stannin at the jawbox.'

job, illegal activity: 'He was out on a job last night. Blew up three shaps anna Cartina.' 'I saw the armalite under his coat so he must be goin out onna job.'

joinin, rebuke, chastise: 'The next time I set eyes on that wee targe I'll give her a good joinin.' 'He give me a terrible joinin when all I was doin was makin faces at him.'

jorum, measure of liquor, depending on the generosity of the pourer: 'Houl on, man, and we'll have a wee jorum.'

jubilant, juvenile: 'She's a jubilant delinquent.'

juke, dodge, elude: 'He juked roun the corner.' 'When its his turn to stan a roun he's a dab haun at jukin ye.'

juke-the-beetle, poor cook: 'Her champ's always full of lumps. The woman's just a juke-the-beetle.'

juke-the-bottle, teetotaller: 'Don't be astin him along. He's onny an oul juke-the-bottle.'

jundered, jostled: 'He jundered his way through. I nearly went harp six on the flure.'

kack-handed, left-handed, awkward: 'He's no carpenter and nivver was. He's that kack-handed you wouldn't credit it.'

kaileyin, party-going, having a good time, going from one ceilidhe to another, gossiping: 'All he does is go kaileyin every night.' 'She's been kaileyin every night for the last month.' 'Her tongue nivver stops. All she thinks of its kaileyin.'

ken, 1. know, be acquainted with: 'A ken him well.' 'He came intil our ken a good wee while back.' 2. utensil used for making tea, esp. by shipyardmen: 'I'll boil yir ken for ye.'

kent, had knowledge of: 'A kent him well.' 'A kent John for the last forty year.' See **ken.**

kep, 1. flat-topped forage cap with a straight peak: 'His kep blew aff in the gale.' 2. retain: 'A kep it because he gave it to me.'

kidleys, kidneys: 'Alec's having bother with his kidleys. It's the drink.'

kileery, light-headed: 'She's a wee kileery. Hasn't an ounce.'

kitchen, comfort: 'Butter to butter's no kitchen' (said of two girls dancing together).

kitterdy, giddy, foolish person: 'She's nathin but a wee kitterdy.'

knawky, cunning, crafty: 'Keep your eyes skinned. She's as knawky as the divil himself.'

knee-cap, terrorist punishment, on suspected informers, by shooting victims in both knees: 'Wee Sammy's been knee-capped twice. He's had a terrible time of it, the sowl.'

know-all, superior person, someone who knows everything: 'Her? She's an oul know-all.' 'If anybody can put ye right it's Cissy. She's the know-all of the family.'

knowin, small amount, what you would know to be there: 'Cud ye lennus a wee knowin of sugar?'

kyart, 1. horse drawn vehicle: 'If you don't watch out you'll cowp the oul kyart intil the sheugh.' 'Keep yer eye out fir thon corner or you'll cowp the kyart, load an all.' 2. difficulty, dilemma: 'The man has the mine of a wee lad. I knew he'd finish up in the kyart.'

 **lacin,** beating: 'He gave the wee lad a quare lacin.' 'My da give me a lacin for scuffin my new shoes.'

lack, like, similar to: 'Lack ye know.' 'The wee lad's awful lack his farr's side of the house.'

laid up, unwell, confined to bed with illness: 'He's been laid up this fortnight.' 'Seeing she's laid up I'll hafta get her a buncha grapes.'

lake, leak: 'The teacher asked her what a lake was and she said it was a hole in a kettle.'

lally, lollipop: 'The child was flaffin her lally all over her good new dress.'

larn, teach, acquire knowledge, study: 'That'll larn ye nivver for till do that again.' 'She's goin till night classes till larn French.' 'The wee lad always brings out his books when I tell him he hasta larn his lessons.'

larry, delivery vehicle, truck: 'I got them for next to nathin. They fellaffa larry.' 'The wee fella fellafa larry an hurt himself.'

lat, large amount: 'He gave me a quare lat.' 'It takes a quare lat of ijits to fill Windsor Park.'

lather, ladder: 'The winda cleaner fell aff is lather.'

lennusahaun: request for assistance: 'For God's sake wud ye lennusahaun with this table?'

lennusapoun, request for a loan: 'Ye cudden lennusapoun cud ye? Till Friday?' 'He says to me "Cud ye lennusapoun?" I tole him to get stuffed.'

lenthamatung, reprimand, reproach: 'I give him the lenthamatung. He ast for it.'

leppin, 1. throbbing painfully: 'My corns is leppin.' 'I can't sleep with my sore knee. It starts leppin the minnit I get into bed.' 2. jumping on horseback: 'The mare was fairly leppin.' 'We're going to see the leppin on Saturday.'

lettin in, leaking: 'My shoes are lettin in.'

lettin on, pretending: 'I knew rightly she didn't mean what she said. I knew she was onny lettin on.'

letton, reveal, disclose: 'Nivver letton ye saw me.' 'He knew but he nivver letton.'

liarintit, invitation to begin a meal, eat heartily: 'Liarintit. It'll warm the cockles of yir heart.' 'See my man? Make him a fog feed and ye don't have to tell him to liarintit.'

lift, understand, grasp the meaning of: 'She's onny two but that wee girl can lift me.' 'I listened to him for ires but I cudden lift a single word.'

lifted, 1. arrested, taken into custody by police: 'He was lifted twice in the one week.' 'The peelers must be sick of the sight of him. They lifted him again last night.' 2. assisted, helped up after a fall: 'Listen and I'll explain what happened. Dickey was lifted, but he wasn't taken to any police barracks. He was lifted because he fell.'

lig, fool, light-hearted person: 'She's always actin the lig.'

like hisself, little changed, of normal appearance: 'I was up lookin at the corpse. He's awful like hisself.' 'She was bad for a long time but when I saw her in the coffin she was awful like herself.'

likkinapramise, clean a room hastily, incompletely: 'I give the house a likkinapramise.' 'Just give the flure a likkinapramise until we get back.'

lilties, people who act foolishly, irresponsibly: 'I saw the two of them goin down the road like a perr of lilties that didden know day from night.'

lion upstairs, in bed, not yet awake: 'Wud ye luck at the time and him still lion upstairs.' 'Lion upstairs? That's a question to ask at levin in the morning.'

lippit, taste: 'I made him a bowl of onion soup but the oul divil wudden lippit.' 'I offered her panada but she just wudden lippit. Sure I keep telling her to eat it up but it just goes in one ear and out the other.'

loaf, intelligence, awareness: 'Use yer loaf, man.' 'You get nowhere in this world if you don't use yer loaf.'

lock, considerable amount, not a small quantity: 'She gave me a good lock of them beans.' 'I ast him to give me a lock of his spuds.'

long, to desire, to yearn for happier times: 'Are you thinkin long?' 'She just sits there thinkin long. What good does that do anybody?'

lose, undo, unfasten: 'I told him not to forget to lose his laces before he wenta bed.'

low set, small of stature: 'She's a wee low set woman. When she sits down ye wudden know she was there.'

luck, stare at, behold: 'She gave me a luck that wud have turned milk.' 'Wud ye just luck at the way that woman's dressed.'

lump, growing child: 'She's a great wee lump.' 'He's a big lump of a lad now.'

maddles, term used in dressmaking and millinery trades: 'We cud do with some younger maddles.' 'Her and her sister are maddles ni but they haven't been maddlin long.' 'That hat is one of our latest wee maddles.'

make trex, bid farewell, depart after a visit: 'Slate. I'll hafta make trex.'

male, meal; breakfast, lunch, tea or dinner: 'She's a great one for four males a day.' 'He expects to see a male on the table the mint he walks in through the door.'

mands biz friz, indicates extreme cold: 'Luck at them. Mands biz friz so they are.' 'If onny I'd brought my gloves for mands biz friz.'

mane, miserly, lacking in generosity: 'Ye wudden credit how mane that fella is.' 'Mister you're on the mane road to Ballymena and the nearer you get to it the maner it gets.'

mangey, 1. skin disease in animals: 'The cat's mangey.' 2. mean, miserly: 'Don't expect anything from him. He's terrible mangey.' See **mingey.**

mantanny, aunt named Annie: 'Mantanny wud nivver ast ye if ye had a mouth on ye.' 'Mantanny won prizes at the dancin when she was a wee girl. She's very light on her feet.'

marley, marble, used in the game of marbles: 'He lost his marley down a gratin.' 'He cried his wee eyes out when he cudden fine his marley.'

meelcartins, chilblains: 'My heart's scalded with the meelcartins.'

meetin, church service: 'I ast her if she was for meetin and she gave me a look.' 'That was a great preacher at the meetin this morning. Ye cud have felt the spits of him five pews away.'

meggs, eggs of the domestic hen: 'I always like meggs hard.' 'I ast her to fry meggs for my breakfast.'

melt, indefinite part of the human body: 'I'll knock yer melt in so I will.' 'He got intil a fight and got his melt knocked in. He was good value for it.'

mended, improved in health, recovered from illness: 'Our bootmaker's awful well mended for he was at death's dure.'

minchin, trespassing: 'He keeps minchin intil our feel.'

mine, 1. remember: 'I forgot to mine my parcel.' 'D'ye mine the day we all went up the Cavehill fir a picnic an it poured?' 2. take care of, look after: 'I ast her to mine the shap.' 3. opinion, viewpoint: 'Sure he doesn't know his own mine.' 4. give heed to: 'Nivver mine him. He's nat worth botherin about.' 5. apply oneself to: 'Mine yer own business.' 6. take objection to: 'Ye wudden mine callin roun wud ye?' 7. observe, take note of: 'Mine the step.' 'Mine where ye're goin.' 8. belonging to me: 'What's his is mine and what's mine's me own.'

minexore, indicates neck pain (as distinct from 'pain in the neck'): 'I can't turn roun for minexore.'

mingey, mean, uncharitable, ungenerous: 'She's awful mingey. She wudden even give you the time of day.' 'She's that mingey they call it Christmas mourn in her house.'

mint, short period of time: 'The train goes in a couple of mints.' 'Houl yir horses. I'll onny be a mint.' 'The mint I set eyes on you I remembered.'

mismorrowed, ill-matched: 'If ivver two people were mismorrowed, it's them two.'

mizzle, mild rain: 'It's started to mizzle.' 'This wire wud senn ye roun the bend. It'll start to mizzle any minnit.' 'I'd left my umbrella in to be restrung and there I was, caught in the mizzle.'

monmone, unaccompanied: 'I didden come to the dance with anybody. I'm monmone.'

monney down, just out of bed: 'I'm not at myself yet. Sure monney down.' See **monney up.**

monney up, just out of bed: 'Monney up this mint.' 'Wait till I get my brain shired. Monney up.' See **monney down.**

morr, female parent: 'I'll hafta ast m'morr if she'll let me go to the party.' 'M'morr isn't up outa her bed yet.'

morrowin, borrowing a horse on the understanding that it will be returned the following day; harvest-time custom: 'I've been morrowin with Wullie John now for many a long day.' 'Onny for the morrowin I wudden know where I was.'

morr tung, native speech: 'When ye hear the morr tung in yer ears ye know yer among frens.' 'The best thing about goin home on a visit is to be able till lissen till people usin their morr tung.'

mouthful, small amount, cupful, tea not taken formally at the table: 'Wud ye like a mouthful in yer haun?' 'I'm not stayin. I'll just have a mouthful in my haun.'

mower, more, additional quantity, extra helping: 'There's mower tea in the pot if you want any.' 'You remember that song, "The Mower We Are Together"?'

muncle, brother of the speaker's father or mother: 'Muncle's a quare boyo.' 'Muncle give me a poun for my birthday.'

mutton dummies, plimsolls, gym shoes: 'Imagine! Tryin to play futball in his mutton dummies!'

51

**nackitaff,** stop, desist, cease: 'I tole her to nackitaff but she wudden heed me.'

nammel jug, vessel made of enamel: 'The great thing about a nammel jug is that it doesn't break if you drap it.' 'Nammel jugs always make me think of ospill.'

nattalat, small, insignificant quantity: 'What am I growin in the garden. Ack, nattalat.' 'There's nattalat in the paper the night.'

nearall, mainly, mostly: 'That tea was nearall water.' 'We'll call the meetin to order. We're nearall here ni.'

neb, nose: 'She isn't a bad sort onny she can't help puttin her neb in.' 'Every time he sneezes ye can hear his neb crakin like a whip.' 'He cud hoke a path with his neb from here till Ballyclare an nivver get a mote in his eye.'

nebby, inquisitive (usually applied to a busybody): 'She's terrible nebby.'

neg, 1. food used for making omelettes: 'It's hard to bate a neg in the pan.' 'She ast me what way I'd like a neg and I said with anor one.' 2. scold, rebuke constantly: 'She's onny an oul neg.'

neggin, 1. scolding, persistently finding fault: 'The wife nivver staps neggin me.' 2. throbbing, insistent pain or problem: 'This oul tooth kept neggin all night.' 'It's been neggin me ivver since whether I done the right thing.'

neighbour, indicates agreement with a proposed action, that it is no bother: 'It's all right. Sure it's neighbour.'

neuck, take without permission, steal: 'I saw the wee lad neuck one of the apples.'

ni, at the present, the present time: 'I'm goin ni.' 'Ni is the hour, as the song says.'

nire, 1. not either: 'She's isn't goin an nire am I.' 2. sixty minutes: 'I'll see ye in about a nire.' 'I've been stannin here waitin a nire so I have.' 'I was poundin roun the shaps for a nire and my feet just give up.'

nire hiltner hairaff, no sign of, no sight of: 'I lucked high an low but there was nire hilter hare of him.' 'I let the wee lad out two seconds ago an ni there's nire hiltner hairaff him.' 'Where that wee dug gets to I don't know but when I lucked there was nire hiltner hairaff him.'

nivverbor, suggests you should change your mind, take a different course of action, or do nothing: 'Nivverbor yir head.' 'If you're a wise man you'll nivverbor.' 'I tole him to nivverbor but he nivverbord listenin.'

noan, not any: 'I have noan left. They're all done.' 'Monmone in the house. There's noan of them in.'

nocker up, person who acts as professional alarm clock: 'We used to have a great wee nocker up but it was a long while ago. He'd dunder at the door until you riz.'

noddity, eccentric, someone whose behaviour is abnormal: 'I'd say he was a noddity all right. Sure the way he gets on wud show ye he hadda wee bittava want.' 'Imagine, puttin 50p. on a horse called "Fourth". Only a noddity wud do a stupid thing like that.'

no empey skite, well-fed: 'By the look of him that fella's no empey skite.' 'After what he shovelled intil him I wud say he's no empey skite.' 'After a coupla fried eggs an three farls of soda yir no empey skite.'

no goat's toe, judicious, of good sense: 'I know him well. He's no goat's toe I can tell you.'

no gra, without enthusiasm, lacking interest or appetite: 'He had no gra for his dinner.'

nopen woon, unbandaged injury to the flesh caused by blow or stab: 'There was me with a nopen woon and nobody bothered their head.' 'That man of hers has a fice like a nopen woon.'

53

Norn Iron, Northern Ireland: 'When the man called me a footer I knew I was in Norn Iron.'

nyarley fry, well-cooked fry of eggs, sausages, bacon, and soda bread: 'Ye cudden bate a nyarley fry.' 'Once he gets stuck intil a nyarley fry he's neighbour.'

nyrps, depressing thoughts, low spirits: 'That woman always gives me the nyrps.'

oan, possess: 'I don't oan this bisileek. I was lent it.'

odious, unusual, distinctive, marked: 'That's an odious fine day so it is.' 'She's an odious fine woman.'

orchin, small boy, mischievous youngster: 'He's a terrible wee orchin.' 'The wee orchin neucked an orange.'

ornje, gold-coloured citrus fruit: 'Ye cudden bate one of them chaffa ornjes.' 2. colour between red and yellow: 'I ast for a pair of ornje men's socks an the girl give me a look.'

orrday, recently, a few days ago: 'I saw her the orrday.' 'I heard about it the orrday there.'

orrdure, alternative entrance or exit: 'There was a bumskerr and we all hadda use the orrdure.' 'There was a notice that said "Use orrdure".'

ospill, place of healing: 'She's lyin in the Satty Ospill.' 'She was tuck to ospill in an amblence.' 'When you ast in the ospill they onny luck at ye. All I wanted was to fine the cherry octopus to see about my feet.'

oul, 1. ancient, venerable: 'He's a right oul age.' 'She's an oul ijit.' 'Ye cudden help but like the oul cratur.' 2. held in high regard: 'I bought this bit of an oul coat only last week. I wudden be without it.'

oulig, old fool, aged idiot: 'He's an oulig. Ye'd think he'd know better at his time of life.'

oulip, abuse, insult: 'Don't be givvin me any of yer oulip.'

oxtercog, assist by holding under the arms: 'We hadda oxtercog the oul blether the whole way home.'

oxters, armpits: 'That wee woman's in debt up till her oxters.' 'Honest to Gawd, Harry, I'm up the creek up till my oxters.'

pahle, limp, move with difficulty, travel slowly and laboriously on foot: 'He's a rare sight tryin to pahle up the stairs.' 'Take it from me, Willie's nathin but a pahle. There's more life in Willie's walking stick than there is in Willie.' 'I'll pahle down till your house the night for a wee bit of yer crack.'

Pakkies, natives of Pakistan: 'After the wee Pakkie sole me a strip of carpet for my back passage I tole him I hoped his sore head wud be better soon.' 'Them turbines the Pakkis wear must make their heads awful warm when it's a hot day.'

palaver, debate, to talk at length, to discuss in tedious detail: 'All I got was a whole palaver about it.' 'Him and her spent the whole night on a long palaver.'

pan, 1. cooking utensil used for frying: 'The wife gives me the pan for breakfast seven days a week.' 'My sister had her stummick out last week and now she can ate anything. Last night she even had the pan.' 2. human face: 'If you don't mine yer language I'll knock yer pan in.' 'She has a pan like a ploughed field.'

panada, bread pudding: 'She's that bad all she can ate is panada.' 'Since I got my new teeth I've been livin on panada. It's cummin outa my ears.'

pant, absurd activity: 'Did you see the pant at the corner last night?' 'There was a right pant when he walked into the house futless.'

parletic, intoxicated, thoroughly inebriated: 'He was measurin the walls last night again. Parletic up to the oxters.'

parmacy, chemist's shop: 'I'm away down to the parmacy to get some jube jubes for meers for we're flyin to London.' 'While I'm out I'll drap in at the parmacy for some moth balls for my drawers.'

parritch, popular breakfast food made by boiling oatmeal or other cereal into a thick paste: 'My man's dyin about a plate of parritch for his breakfast.' 'That wee lad has my heart broke. He won't lip his parritch.'

part, tropical bird with brilliant plumage: 'They had a part in a cage that cud say "I wanta drink".' 'My man's away out till buy seed for the part. That oul bird costs a fortune.'

passremarkin, describes a person apt to make uncomplimentary comments about others: 'I don't like her at all. She's awful pass-remarkin.'

pass yerself, behave sociably, act amiably when in company: 'I'll just have a wee drink to pass myself.'

pavilion passenger, rider on a motor-cycle pillion: 'She was his pavilion passenger when he ran intil the lamp-post.' 'It's grate fun ridin on the pavilion but it fairly ruins yer herr.'

pech, grunt, pant: 'She was pechin up the stairs.' 'The pechs of her! Ye cud hev heard them a mile away.'

pechlin, see **pahle.**

perr, a couple, husband and wife: 'There's her and her ma an they're a perr.' 'The perr of them went down the street like a couple of lilties.'

persperatin, sweating: 'I was fairly persperatin. The swate was pourin aff me.'

phrase, a stage, change, period of time: 'She's goin through one of her phrases.'

picker, person with poor appetite, one who prefers small helpings: 'I'd far rarr cook fer a gorb than a picker any day.'

58

piece, a worker's packed lunch: 'I got him a wee plastic beg for him to carry his piece to work.' 'He's as fussy as the day and the morra about what's in his piece.'

piggin, unclean, untidy: 'Her house is always piggin. That wumman doesn't know what a brush is for.'

piggy, street game played with small, pointed piece of wood which is propelled through the air by a stick: 'I tole the wee lads if that oul piggy went through one of my windas they'd pay for it.'

pig's back, on top of the world; indicates confidence, absolute assurance: 'After ten minnits' play the team was on the pig's back, two goals up.'

pijun-futted, sly, cunning: 'Watch that one. She's pijun futted.'

pijuns, birds of the dove family: 'He's been breedin pijuns all his life.' 'Life isn't worth livin since the man next dure started breedin pijuns. Sure they breed like rabbits.'

pitcher, film, movie: '*Gone With The Wine*'s a pitcher and a half. I cried my eyes out.' 'The big pitcher was terrible; it was a waste av good money quein up till see it.'

plane, to be involved in recreational activity, taking part in a game: 'The wee lad's out plane in the street.' 'The childer were plane tig all day.'

plaster, hypocrite: 'He's nathin but an oul plaster.' See **poultice.**

plite, courteous, well-behaved: 'He's awful plite. Pulls up his trousers when he sits down.' 'He's an obligin, plite wee man.' 'I've nivver met a plite rent collector in my whole life.'

plowterin, moving aimlessly about, acting without any particular purpose, wasting time: 'Ack, I'm onny plowtering aroun.' 'He's plowterin away there in the garden.'

Plues, Linfield Football Club: 'The wee Plues can fairly play.' 'The Plues is plane away the day.'

plugher, 1. indication of lung infection, to clear the throat noisily: 'He has an awful bad plugher.' 'Ye should hear the plughers of her. Bad chests run in the family.' 2. smoky, dusty atmosphere: 'There was a terrible plugher in the room for he was at his oul pipe.'

plump, sudden shower of rain: 'That was a right plump. I was wringin when I got home.'

plute, pester, annoy, aggravate: 'The chile's been plutin me all day.' 'That wee lad plutes the life outa me.'

potata clock, around eight a.m. or p.m.: 'Seeya potata clock.'

poultice, hypocrite: 'She's nathin but an oul poultice, that's what I think.'

powerful, likeable, unusual: Her husband's a powerful wee man. Ye cudden help but take to him.' 'The new minister's a powerful preacher but it's nice when he gets to thirdly.' ('Thirdly' relates to the preaching convention of having first, second and third points of progression in the discourse.)

pravins, province: 'I've been livin in the pravins all my life.' 'It wud sicken ye sometimes. The wire's that bad over the whole pravins.'

preys, potatoes: 'Them preys was lovely.' 'She give me a great plate of preys.'

prig, to make a bargain: 'If ye go to Ballymena and ye don't prig they'll think ye're mad.' 'Unless ye prig ye'll pay through the nose.'

puke, 1. to vomit, to spew: 'She was pukin all over the place. The meal didden agree with her.' 2. supercilious person, one who displays superior airs: 'She's a right puke.' 'She looked through me, the puke.'

pumlican, owner of licensed premises: 'He's a pumlican. Sure he owns two pubs.'

pumpture, motoring misfortune, tyre trouble: 'We were onny down the road ten minutes when he gatta pumpture.' 'He was in a right state when he gat his third pumpture in two days.'

purr down, refers to the movement of furniture, term used by removal men: 'Purr down ni, Jimmy.' 'Ye didden purr down when I told ye to purr down. I nearly busted a gut. What kine of a man are ye?'

puttin onner, getting dressed: 'She was onny puttin onner when I called roun.' 'The wife's upstairs puttin onner.'

quare, memorable, unusual, outstanding: 'You're a quare geg.' 'The pitcher was a quare bittava laugh.' 'It was a quare wet day. I was foundered.'

quare man m' da, indicates disbelief, an awareness that an attempt is being made to fool the hearer: 'Sole yer house? Quare man m' da!' 'Won the pools, did ye? Quare man m' da.'

Quewy, affectionate version of 'Hugh'. See **Shewy.**

quilt, objectionable, mean or disobliging person: 'She's a quilt of the deepest dye.' 'If ye want my opinion Rachel's a born quilt.' 'A quilt of the first water, that fella. He has an eye like a cold fried egg.' 'The woman's a right oul quilt. She's as cuttin as a pan loaf.'

quire, band of singers: 'She's fairly come on. She's singin in the quire ni.' 'Mary's goin with a quare nice fella. He says he's in the quire.'

ramstam, act recklessly, thoughtlessly: 'He went at it ramstam.' 'I warned the man. I tole him not to go at it ramstam.'

rapin, harvesting: 'He said he was wore out for he was rapin in the feel all day.' 'She ast him was he busy and when he said he'd been rapin for hours she took till her heels, the silly ijit.'

rare, raise, educate: 'I hadda rare three childer an I wudden do it again.'

rare crack, entertaining, lively conversation: 'It's always rare crack if he's there.' 'It was rare crack at Minnie's last night.'

rare turn, amusing person: 'She's a rare turn. I tuk my dead enn at her.' 'That fella's a rare turn. He had everybody in stitches.'

rarr, prefer: 'I'd far rarr go to the pitchers.' 'I'd rarr ye didden tell her.'

ratten, unfortunate, unpleasant: 'Yir man had a heart attack? Ack that was ratten for ye.' 'She tole me Alec had cut his throat an I said that was ratten for her.'

raut, worked: 'He raut in the shipyard all his life.' 'He nivver raut anywhere else but Mackie's.'

redd, tidy up after a party, clear the table after a meal: 'I havta go an redd up.'

rench, rinse: 'He wudden even help me to rench the dishes.' 'I can't talk to ye ni. I havta rench the clothes out.'

rentin, vomiting: 'She was rentin the night out.' See **puke.**

riftin, belching: 'We got that much to ate the ould fella was riftin like mad.'

right, used to add emphasis to a statement: 'That's a right bittava night.'

right haun, mess or muddle: 'The dog made a right haun of the garden. One of these days I'm goin to show it my boot.' 'John made a right haun of the back room. He wasted more paint than he put on.'

right ijit, stupid, senseless person: 'Charlie's a right ijit.' 'I tole him he acted like a right ijit when they ast him to stann up an sing.'

rightly, 1. merry, intoxicated: 'When I saw him he was rightly.' 'Him? Two drinks and he's rightly.' 'That fella wud get rightly on a tummler of tomato juice.' 2. prospering: 'Now he's workin he's doin rightly.'

right 'n' bad, in poor health, in a serious condition (not a reference to poor handwriting): 'I tuk him a buncha grapes for he was right 'n' bad.' 'I tole the chemist I was right 'n' bad and he said did I want a new ballpoint. Imagine!'

right one, unpredictable person: 'Keep yer eyes skinned. That boy's a right one.' 'I knew she was a right one the minnit she opened her mouth.'

right shar, fairly heavy fall of rain: 'That was a right shar. It's a good job I brought my raincoat.'

right yar, indicates agreement, approbation: ' "Ye can go on ahead." "Right yar." ' ' "See ye Sardy?" "Right yar." '

right yebe, sign of approval: 'Right yebe, Charlie. That's just dandy.' 'Ye're all right ni? Right yebe.'

rining, raining: 'It's been rining since I got up.' 'That's what's the matter with this place. It's always rining. It nivver staps.'

riotery, noisy pigs and geese in a farmyard: 'The riotery was shackin.' 'You shudda heard the riotery. It was worse than a disco.'

ritefy, confirm: 'I said I wudden pay it until he sut down to ritefy the figures.' 'Ye can't say it'll do until you get him to ritefy it.'

riz, out of bed: 'She wassent even riz when I called at the house after ten.'

rosiner, drink, a good measure of whiskey: 'You'll have a rosiner before ye go?' 'That was a right rosiner. Here's t'ye.'

rowboat, robot used by bomb disposal experts for testing purposes: 'They sent a rowboat out to see if it was a bomb an it was nathin but a hoax.'

rumplety thump, untidily, in disorder: 'She just left everythin rumplety thump.'

runt, a cabbage stalk; the weakling in a litter of pigs; undersized **person:** 'I can take a salad but not when there's a coupla runts in it.' 'He's only a wee runt of a man.'

 **sack,** unwell, indisposed: 'I was aff sack for a whole week.' 'She's been on the sack for more nor a month.'

saft day, mild weather: 'It's that kine of day, saft.'

sallrite, indicates that all is well: 'There's nathin to worry about. I saw the house. Sallrite.' 'I hadda a luck at the new car. Sallrite, sotis.'

sally wattle, branch from a thorn hedge with the thorns removed: 'We were walkin down the loanin swishin our sally wattles.'

Sardy, Saturday: 'Are ye goin till the match on Sardy? It'll onny be a waste of good money but sure ye nivver know.'

sarky, speak ironically: 'I can't stann him, he's that sarky.'

sauncy, lively, full of fun: 'She's a sauncy wee thing. Ye cudden keep pace with her.'

sawn, an affirmative statement, indicates that a proposal will be carried out: 'Member what they were sayin about an excursion? Sawn.'

scald, tea: 'Come on on in an we'll have a wee drap av scald.'

scalded, troubled, distressed: 'My heart's scalded with that wee lad.'

scaldy, hairless: 'The wee lad lucks terrible scaldy after gettin his hair cut.'

scrake, beginning: 'She was up at the scrake av dawn.' 'The party went on all night. We gat home at the scrake av dawn. You shudda heard the birds.'

scrapins, 1. delicate, badly failed: 'She's away to scrapins. It's a pity of the woman.' 2. left-overs: 'There's nathin in the fridge but two or three scrapins.'

scretch, wound caused by a sharp object: 'I gotta scretch on my haun when I tried to stroke the oul cat.'

screw, grown: 'Look at the size of the wee lad, wud ye? Isn't he gettin big? Screw outa all proportions.'

scringe, to grind the teeth noisily: 'There I was scringin my teeth and the wife said it kep her awake.' 'The dentist said I'd scringed my teeth down till the gums.' 'I tole the wee lad nat till scringe his teeth but ye might as well talk till the wall.'

scrub, scoundrel, untrustworthy person: 'I knew from the word go that fella was a scrub.' 'He's a scrub but he gets on as if he was roilty or somethin.'

scrunch, sound made when walking on gravel: 'He was scrunchin up the garden path.'

scuff, showing signs of use: 'I tole the wee lad to watch he didden scuff his new shoes.' 'He went to Sunday school and came back with his new suit all scuffed. Ye cudden be up to them.'

scum, announces that an expected parcel has arrived: 'Mary, that frock you sent fer. Scum.' 'John, wud ye go to the dure? It's the oil. Scum.'

scunner, dislike, resent: 'I took a scunner at him after he called me names.'

scut, untrustworthy, unreliable person: 'That's a scut if ivver I saw one.' 'He's a scut of the first water.'

scuttle, British Airways' Belfast-London service: 'The only way to go to London is on the scuttle.'

sedsamarley, liable to act senselessly: 'See him? Sedsamarley. Take it from me.'

sedscut, insensible, capable of foolish behaviour: 'I know the fella well. Sedscut.'

Seeinawa, the Belfast branch of the C & A department store: 'I said I'd see him outside Seeinawa's.'

seeya, a parting greeting, confirms a future appointment: 'Seeya, Charlie. Orra bess.' 'Seeya Sardy.' See **seeyearoun**.

seeyearoun, a parting greeting, expressing an expectation of a future unspecified meeting: 'Cheerio fer ni. Seeyearoun.' See **seeya**.

sempy, the opposite of full: 'Luk at my glass, Alec, sempy.'

senfer, signifies a narrow or lucky escape: 'When the car whizzed past me I thought I was senfer.' 'When I swalleyed that bone I was sure I was senfer.'

sevendible, strong, sound: 'He's a sevendible wee man.'

sex, tea-time in Ballymena: 'What do you want to know what we do about sex for? Sure that's when we have our tea.'

sex mechanics, sexual offenders: 'The papers is full of sex mechanics these days. Make ye sick.' 'I've stapt buyin a paper on Sunday. Ye get nathin but sex mechanics.'

shade, 1. hair parting: 'If you wear yir bare head you'll get your shade wrecked. It's quaren windy.' 2. farmyard barn: 'He's put the ladder in the shade.'

shamrock tea, weak tea (implies it was brewed with three leaves): 'All she ivver gives ye is shamrock tea. It's like drinkin water.'

shappin, process of buying necessities: 'I'm wore out shappin.' 'Shappin's awful hard on the oul feet.'

shar, 1. shower or rain: 'That was a right bittava shar I got myself caught in.' 2. group of people, usually of doubtful character: 'The wee lad's got himself in with a right shar. One of them dyes his hair.' 'That was a right shar you were at the dance with. I wudden give one of them an inch.'

sheesahedonner, able, intelligent person: 'That one's no fool. Sheesahedonner.' 'Sheesahedonner. That's why she was able to bate the man down to two poun from five for that sofa.'

sheugh, ditch: 'She fell intil a sheugh and she has thorns in her yit.'

Shewy, affectionate form of 'Hugh': 'I'm going to get Shewy a blazer with the initial "S" on it.' See **Quewy**.

shillitonme, to be attacked verbally, castigated: 'I was hardly through the door before shillitonme like a hundred of breeks.' 'I'll have to run, Harry. I'm half an hour late already. I was onny ten minutes late last night and ye shuddav seen the way shillitonme.'

shinyit, inquires if the lady of the house has returned: 'Shinyit? If she isn't I'll call back after.'

shired, cleared, refreshed: 'I want to get my head shired. I wasn't in bed till all hours.'

shizawed, indicative of eccentricity: 'Shizawed all right. Ye wudden know what she'll do next.' 'When she ast the man paintin the white lines on the road if he ever foun hisself in a corner, I said to myself, Gawd shizawed.'

shoon, footwear: 'The girl in the shop said she had a woman in an God Almighty cudden fit her feet. She said she cudden get the woman's shoon outa her head.'

shout, enquiries if the lady of the house has gone out: 'Shout? I wanted to have a wee word with her.'

shugglyshoe, shake: 'The car won't start. Cummun help me to give it a good shugglyshoe.'

shup, enquires if the lady of the house is out of bed: 'Shup yet? Mebbe I shud come back?'

shuttyer gub, shut up: 'That's what's wrong with the wumman. She won't listen when ye say to her shuttyer gub.' 'I said to her wud ye shuttyer gub and she clapsed.'

shuvaff, direction to clear off, go away: 'I tole him to shuvaff but he nivver budged.'

sickassadawg, extremely unwell: 'The wee chile gorbed herself that much at the social that she was sickassadawg.' 'Since I ate them mushrooms I've been sickassadawg. I wunner what was in them?'

sickner, disappointment, failure to come up to expectations: 'I got a right sickner when the horse came in last.' 'I got a bittava sickner when he said he was a married man.'

simmit, undervest: 'He's very cowlrife. He wears his simmit all summer.'

singed, clean, wash out: 'I got meers singed yesterday and I can't hear a thing.' 'Ever since I got meers singed they're givin me gippo.'

skelly, 1. glare, fixed look: 'She did nathin but skelly at me the whole night.' 2. cross-eyed: 'He has an awful skelly. The trouble was I didden know and ast him to go where he was lookin.'

skelp, blow, strike, physically chastise: 'If you don't behave I'll give you a skelp across the gub.' 'I give him a skelp and that soon brought him to his senses.'

skelph, splinter: 'I gotta skelph in my finger. It's still sower.'

skiff, light shower of rain: 'Sonnya wee skiff.'

skinnymalink, unduly thin person: 'If that wee skinnymalink hadda couple of holes in her back she'd make a right flute.'

skinnymalink meledeon legs, old-time expression of irreverence or ridicule, used by small boys concerning an elder whom they want to humiliate, esp. if the person is unduly thin: 'Ma, skinnymalink meledeon legs chased us again, so he did.'

skint, 1. penniless, broke: 'Cud ye lennus a coupla poun? I'm skint.' 2. describes intense cold: 'It wud have skint ye, it was that coul.'

skite, 1. blow with the fist: 'He give me a right skite on the face.' 2. drinking bout: 'I saw him measurin the walls. He's on the skite again.' 3. short journey: 'She tuk a wee skite down till the grocer's.' 'We went for a skite in the new car.'

skite-the-gutter, person of no account: 'Don't take any notice of him. He's onny a skite-the-gutter.'

skitter, untrustworthy, contemptible person: 'He's a skitter if ivver there was one.'

slap, gap in hedge or fence: 'I saw him abin the slap. He was stovin.'

slate, opposite of early: 'Slate. What kep ye?'

sleekit, sly, devious: 'That woman's a sleekit rat. Just you be careful.' 'She's that sleekit she wud hardly tell ye the right time.'

sleutery, limp, lifeless: 'Ye wudden take to him. He gives ye a terrible sleutery handshake.'

69

slow stamp, not express postage: 'Cud ye givvus a slow stamp for this letter? It's in no hurry.'

sluther, to drink or sup noisily: 'He drives me up the walls the way he sluthers his tea.'

sly spawn, ready-cut loaf: 'I always get a sly spawn for I fine it easier to cut.'

smallikin, beating, thrashing: 'She's lost for a good smallikin.'

smittle, infectious: 'Keep away from her. She has the 'flu and it's terrible smittle.'

sonnyme, a declaration that the speaker is alone, unaccompanied: 'Sawl rite, Sammy. Sonnyme, myself.' 'Wud ye open the dure? Sonnyme.'

sotinnit, comment indicative of hot weather: 'Sotinnit? I'm swatin.' 'Sotinnit? I'm goin to need some dorient.'

sotis, adds emphasis to a statement: 'The wire's terrible sotis. It nivver staps rainin.' '*Sardy Night Fever*'s a great picture sotis.' 'Portrush is lovely for yer hollyers sotis.'

sower, 1. painful: 'I have a sower head so I have.' 'I'm sick, sower an tired of listenin to that man yappin at me.' 2. bitter, sharp-tasting: 'That apple tart she made was that sower it wud straighten screw nails.'

spadger, sparrow: 'Wud ye luk at the darts of that wee spadger. Does ye good.'

spalterin, lame, walking unsteadily: 'There she is, spalterin down till the shap.'

spectin, pregnant. See **spittin at the tongs.**

speeley, climb with agility: 'You shudda seen him speeley up the lamp-post.'

spenser, woollen garment, knitted jacket: 'I tole him to be sure and wear his spenser or he'd be freezin, but he wudden heed me.

spitter, implies that the weather is extremely cold: 'That's a night and a half. Spitter.' 'Put some more coal on the fire there. Spitter.'

spittin, occasional raindrops which often precede a heavy shower: 'A minnit ago it was spittin. Now it's coming down in stair-rods.' 'This morning it was onny spittin. Now it's rainin shoemaker's knives.'

spittin at the tongs, state of pregnancy: 'Ye cud tell rightly. She's spittin at the tongs. I wonder what got intil her.'

spittin image, alike, resemble closely: 'He's the spittin image of his da.' 'Ar wee Charlotte's the spittin image of my sister's girl.'

splittin, very painful: 'My head's splittin, so it is.'

splughins, heavy boots: 'The mud'll be feet deep. Better put on yer splughins.'

spoarin, raining heavily: 'It wus onny a wee shire when I came out but luk at it ni. Spoarin.'

spoiled ratten, spoken of a child of over-indulgent parents: 'That wee lad's spoiled ratten. Luck at the way he's gettin on.'

sprachle, trip, stumble: 'He went a right sprachle intil the ditch. From the roars of him ye'd hev thought he was kilt.'

Spress, 'Daily Express': 'I like the Spress because of what it says.'

spucketin, indicates that it is raining heavily: 'This oul wire's desperit. Spucketin again.' 'Luck at it. Spucketin. That's the third time this week, and we havn't seen Tuesday yit.'

spulpin, mischievious, ill-behaved child: 'He's a right wee spulpin. He wants a good hidin.'

spurtle, tool used for thatching: 'Paddy's a quare haun with the spurtle. He can thatch like a champion.'

squarendeer, implies that a price is unduly high: 'Squarendeer to ask that much for a pair of oul gloves. I'd let my hands go barefoot before I'd pay that for them.'

stain, 1. not moving: 'Are ye stain here for a week or a fortnight?' 2. kidney complaint: 'He has a stain in his kidneys.'

stair-rods, once used to keep stair carpets in position; now an expression indicating a heavy downpour of rain: 'It was spittin at first but then it came down in stair-rods.'

71

staken dentity, erroneous identification: 'I tole the police it was a case of staken dentity but they wudden lissen.'

staken ships, popular meal: 'Staken ships fairly sets a man on his feet.' 'The staken ships ye get in Spain nivver taste the same as at home.'

stapt, ceased: 'The clack's stapt.'

stap-the-clack, someone who always expects the worst (from the custom of stopping the clock when there is a death in the house): 'Don't say a word. Here comes stap-the-clack. He'll put a dampener on everything.'

starvin, 1. suffering from extreme cold: 'I'm starvin. Put anor coupla shovelfuls on the fire there.' 2. extremely hungry: 'I'm starvin. I cud ate a horse.'

steemin, 1. raining heavily and consistently: 'You'll need your umberalla. Steemin sotis. Steemin hard.' 2. well intoxicated: 'The last time I set eyes on yer man, steemin just about describes the state he was in.'

stern, 1. mischievious, full of energy: 'The wee girl's very stern. Ye cudden be up to her.' 2. moving: 'Luck at the time it is. Eight o'clock and there's no sign of him stern. He cud sleep till doomsday.' 3. look pointedly: 'He sut stern at me the whole night.'

stikkinout, prominent, impressive, distinguished: 'That goalie was stikkinout.' 'When he gets goin on that flute of his he's stikkinout.'

stime, 1. smallest conceivable object: 'That's a terrible night. I can't see a stime.' 'Lennus a match wud ye? I just can't see a stime.' 2. a chosen moment, refers to the present: 'Stime we were on our way.' 'Stime I had something to eat.'

stocious, inebriated: 'Ack, the man's stocious again. He just can't hole his drink.'

stoonin, causing pain, painful: 'My Gawd but my corn's stoonin.' See **leppin.**

stour, dust, smoke: 'The soot came down the chimley and the stour was awful.' 'The people next dure lit a fire in their garden and ye shudda seen the stour.'

stovin, inebriated: 'He was as full as the Boyne. Just stovin.'

strew, honestly, in truth: 'Strew. It's not a word of a lie.' 'Strew. As Gawd's my witness.'

striffin, thin film inside an egg shell: 'She spreads the butter as thin as striffin.'

stringa misery, doleful, cheerless person: 'Ivver since he had that wet holiday he's been nathin but a stringa misery.'

strunts, displayed when ill-tempered or displeased: 'If I'd knew he took the strunts that easy I'd have give him the go by.'

stry, indicates that it is not raining: 'Thank goodness for that. Ye won't need yer raincoat. Stry.' 'Stry an it's a good job for I left my umbrella in to be restrung.'

stupa ijit, silly person: 'Ye cud sum him up in two words. Stupa ijit.' See **ijit, buckijit.**

suckey up, flatter, compliment insincerely: 'Ye needn't suckey up till me. I can see through ye.' 'Ye can suckey up there till ye're blue in the face. I'm not as green as I'm cabbage-lookin.'

sufficiency, adequate quantity: 'I'll not have another bite, thanks very much. I've had a good sufficiency.'

sughan, apron: 'Put on yer sughan an we'll do the dishes.' 'That wee wumman's a great cook. She'll be caught dead in her sughan.'

Sullen Iron, Republic of Ireland: 'He comes from Sullen Iron. Ye cud tell the minute he opens his mouth.' 'When she said to me, "Denise is six", I knew she was from Sullen Iron.'

Sunny, Sunday, the Sabbath: 'We go to wer church every Sunny morn.' 'If it's a Sunny morn he likes to spend it in his bed.'

swarm, proclamation of warm weather: 'Swarm day, I'll say that for it.' 'Swarm, an me still wearin my woolie vest.'

sweat, indicates that it is raining: 'Luck at that wire, wud ye? Sweat, as usual.'

swithers, indicates indecision: 'I'm in swithers whether I should go or not.' 'She's still in swithers about takin the job.'

 **tara,** terrible: 'That day's wile tara so it is.'

tare, drinking bout: 'It's terrible for her. Her man's on the tare again.' 'Harry's been on the tare for the last week. He's a turn.'

tarred, weary: 'I'm tarred out soam. I've been on the go since early morn.' 'Him? Sure if he onny strikes a match he's tarred out.'

tattie oaten, potato-bread made with oatmeal: 'A coupla farls of fried tattie oaten and he wudden call the Queen his cousin.'

tavishun, device enabling distant events to be watched on a small screen: 'He's stuck in front av the tavishun the whole night.' 'One of these days he'll be caught dead watchin tavishun.'

tea out, a restaurant meal: 'She just loves tea out when she comes up from the country.'

telt, informed: 'Mary telt me about it and so did Aggy. It must be right.'

tension, attention: 'They tole me to ring for tension but nobody came.' 'I hate that shap. They doan pay ye any tension.'

tent, small amount: 'I wunner if ye cud lennus a wee tent of sugar?'

tep, gratuity: 'Boys, shud we gie the waitress a tep?' 'If ye give the taxi man a tep wud he gie ye onny change?'

terraced, man of violence: 'I wudden go up there. You'll onny get a terraced bomb up yir backside.' 'The terraced bombs were goin aff all night.'

terrs, indicates haste: 'Ye shudda seen the terrs of him down the street.' 'The terrs of her to get to the disco—it was outa this world.'

thants, relations: 'We were up at thants for wir tea.' 'Thants want to come with us on our holidays.' 'He says he'd like to go and see thants in Tranta.'

Tharches, road junction in East Belfast: 'There's some good shaps at Tharches.' 'I offen wonder why they call them Tharches when Tharches wus knacked down years ago.'

thashes, remnants of a fire: 'They threw thee sanitary bombs in the dure and thashes wus all that wus left.'

thaveless, incompetent: 'From the luck of her I knew she was thaveless.'

thee, the number above two: 'I'll see ye outside Boots at thee.' 'The thee of us went along togerr.'

themmuns, indicates specific people: 'Themmuns is away Tittaly this year for their holidays. They do themselves awful well.' 'Themmuns an that dog of theirs. They should be in when they're out to hear the row it kicks up.'

therni, 1. recently: 'It onny happened therni.' 'I saw the two of them therni.' 2. expression of sympathy: 'Thereni, chile, you'll soon be better.'

ther thur ther, indicates close proximity: 'Are ye bline? Man dear ther thur ther, the two av them, stannin at the corner.'

thick, 1. extremely friendly, keeping company: 'Him an her's quaren thick this good while.' 2. stupid: 'Sure thon fella's as thick as champ.' 'She's as thick as two planks.'

Thingmy, person whose real name has been forgotten by the speaker: 'Mrs Thingmy was there as large as life and twice as natural.' 'I'm goin to the bingo with Mrs Thingmy. She's awful lucky.'

thissus, inquiry, often heard on a bus: 'I ast fer Chadolly Street. Thissus?'

thon, reference to a person or thing: 'Luck at the far out thon wuns is went in that wee boat.' 'Givvus a quarter of thon carmels at the enn of the shelf.'

thon way, pregnant: 'Charlotte's thon way again. Ye cud take yer enn at her.'

thote, the front of the neck: 'I'm away to the chemist's for some lazenges fer my sore thote.' 'She's drivin me astray in the head. One of these days I'll cut her thote so I will.'

thotherenn, the opposite portion: 'Try thotherenn, Joe. It might be asier to liff if ye try thotherenn.' 'Yir man has flitted. He's livin at thotherenn of the road ni.'

thoutfurrerado, immediately: 'Thoutfurrerado I will now present our chairman with this computer tankard as a wee momentum.'

thout veil, for sure, for certain: 'He said he'd meet me thout veil.' 'I tole you I'd be here thout veil and here am.'

thowaff, to vomit: 'Fer Gawd's sake doan start till thowaff an the flure onny washed.' 'He's a terrible man. Two or thee drinks and before ye know he'll thowaff.'

thowl, ancient: 'Thowl shoes is on their last legs.' 'Thowl coat'll do me my day.'

thrapple, throat: 'I hev an awful pain in my thrapple.' 'I onny went intil the pub to wet my thrapple.'

thrawn, awkward, unco-operative: 'He's a thrawn oul bugger.' 'She's a terrible thrawn chile. She hes me up the walls.'

throng, crowded: 'The town's awful throng this mornin.'

thundergub, noisy, persistent talker: 'Once oul thundergub starts ye can hardly hear yer ears.'

tick, heavy material: 'He shudda put on his tick vest instead of his tin wan. That's why he caught the coul.'

tile, towel: 'They thew in the tile after the secun roun.' 'Mister, I ast ye for tiles for the bathroom, not tiles for the wall. It's tiles to dry your face on I want.

tilet, comfort station: 'Mister, cud ye tellus where the tilet is?' 'I'm luckin fer the tilet. The wee lad's caught short like.'

till, not quite closed: 'Wud ye leave the dure till?'

toe-rag, unreliable person: 'Doan lissen to a word he says. He's a toe-rag of the deepest dye.'

tosh uppers, a chip shop order for two: 'Givvus tosh uppers for me an him.' 'Tosh uppers by the neck there.'

tovy, boastful: 'She'd sicken ye she's that tovy.'

trace, row of houses: 'She lives in one of them trace hices.'

tracter dacter, contractor physician: 'Thon wee tracter dacter talks awful funny. Ye'd think he was firren onny he's black.'

Tranta, Toronto: 'We went to Tranta to see his bror. I didden like it. When ye get a boiled egg ye have to sup it with a wee totie spoon.'

trinket, gutter: 'The stupa ijit drapt his piece in the trinket.'

trinnel, trundle: 'I tole him to go away an trinnel his hoop and give me a minnit's peace.'

truff, stolen articles: 'If ye ast me she has nathin but truff in the house.'

truss, have confidence in: 'I wudden truss that fella as far as I cud see him.' 'Ye cudden even truss her to feed yir budgie.' 'If there's no truss where are ye?'

tuk bad, became unwell: 'He'd be at his warm work onny he tuk bad.' 'She tuk bad in the middle of the sermon. She cudden wait till the hymn.'

tummler, a large drinking-glass: 'I hope somebody'll buy me some of them cut-glass tummlers for Christmas.' 'It's terrible when ye break a good tummler. I've broke three arms myself but when ye break a tummler he gets awful annoyed.'

turbines, headgear: 'Them Pakkies is a funny lot. They wear turbines on their heads.'

twaddel, nonsense: 'She just sat there talkin oul twaddel.' 'All they do at the Corporation is talk a latta twaddel.'

typewriter, secretary: 'This wee girl's a shorthorn typewriter at Stormont. She gets quaren well paid.'

ulster, open sore: 'He's had an operation for an ulster on his stummick.' 'She had a terrible time with her ulster but sure she's gettin over it.'

unbenownced, unaware, unknown: 'That fella won't die unbenownced to hisself. He takes good care of Number One.' 'If that's what happened it's unbenownced to me.' 'Unbenownced to his wife he was livin in sin. Ye wudden credit it.'

unner, beneath, someone lower in grade, fewer than: 'My feet give way unner me.' 'I wudden take her unner my notice.' 'The wee lad's unner thee.'

uppity, snobbish, superior: 'I can't stann that woman she's that uppity.' 'Just because her son's a civil serpent she's that uppity ye'd think she was roilty.'

usent, formerly: 'Usent you to live in Omagh? I've seen you somewhere before.' 'Member when we usent to have proper money, not these oul dismal coins?'

**vannal,** person who causes malicious damage: 'There was a bunch av wee vannals an ye shuda seen what they done.' 'Them vannals set the bus on fire. All they need is a good skelpin.'

venison bline man, a tradesman: 'I ast in the shap where I cud get my hauns on a venison bline man and they lucked at me as if I was away in the head.'

Venna role, a variety of bread: 'Harry's dyin about a slice of toasted Venna role.' 'I always fancy a Venna role if it's fresh.'

verbilly, by word of mouth: 'He didden tell me verbilly. He rung me up on the foam.' 'She spoke to me verbilly in the supermarket about it.'

vialin, string instrument: 'The wee lad's a quare haun with the vialin. Gawd knows who he takes it after.' 'There was a great vialin pler on the bax last night. Thon boy knew how to fiddle.'

vine, conceited: 'She's a vine wee thing.' 'I can't stann that woman. Ye wud wonder what she has to be so vine about.'

vivid, extremely angry: 'When the binmen see all them begs they'll be vivid.' 'She was vivid when she got her stackins all japped.' 'I was vivid when I foun I had walked up till my pew and me with a lather in my tights.'

 **wadden,** cotton wool: 'I tole the chemist I wanted some wadden for meers.'

waitin on, seriously ill: 'He's been waitin on for nearly a fortnight.'

wallace, ballroom dance: 'When he ast me if I was tuk I didden know he could fairly wallace.' 'She's a great wee dancer. The way she could wallace tuk my breath away.'

wance, one time: 'I only ast him the wance.' 'We've onny been in that shop the wance.'

wanes, children: 'Now I can put my feet up and watch *Carnation Street* for the wanes is all in bed.' 'The wanes wud break yer heart but sure ye wudden be without them.' 'Wance the wains is grown up I'll have a wee bitta peace.'

wane the head, loss of reason, temporarily insane: 'Ye cud see he was wane the head when he tole the busman he wanted to go to Dallas with a loada yella man.' 'He's boun to be wane the head if he thinks he can make a livin plane the sexyfoam.'

want, lacking in wit: 'It's a pity of her. She's a noddity. She has a wee want.'

warworks, urinary organs: 'He's in a bad way. He has dodgy warworks.' 'The poor sowl's started to have trouble with his warworks. Ye cudden help but feel sarry for him.'

wattiliware, question seeking advice on choice of dress: 'We'll have to start getting ready but wattiliware?' 'If we're ever going to get to the dance I'll have to make up my mind. Wattiliware?'

wattle, a request for advice: 'Wattle I do if he doesn't turn up?' 'Wattle happen if she says she won't go?'

wed, measure, balance: 'They nivver wed the potatoes. I was flamin.' 'When they wed the bacon it wasn't what it said on the packet.'

wee message, childish mishap: 'Mister wud ye stap the bus? The wee lad's just left a wee message in his seat.'

wee softness, simpleton, slightly retarded: 'Ack am sarry for him. He has a wee softness.'

wee thing, enthusiasm, liking: 'He has a wee thing about singin. Nathin can stap him.' 'He has this wee thing about makin speeches. Ye cudden shut him up.'

well-mended, improved in health: 'After him being so bad he's awful well-mended.' 'He was awful well-mended when I saw him yesterday. He seemed to be awful glad of them grapes.'

wersh, unsalted porridge: 'It turned me when she gave me a plate of wersh.'

wettonus, request to delay, wait for the speaker: 'Wettonus, wud ye?' 'What's all the hurry. Why can't ye wettonus?'

wheeked, snatched: 'She wheeked it outa my haun.'

wheeker, exceptionally good: 'My farr's new car's a wheeker.' 'His drive from the first tee was a wheeker.' 'It was a wheeker of a match. The wee Glens deserved to win.'

wheen, an unspecified number, a quantity (large or small): 'I ast her fer a coupla spuds and she gave me a whole wheen of them.'

wheezle, chest complaint: 'He's had a wee wheezle for two or three days. He needs his chest rubbed.' 'His oul chest's actin up. Ye shud hear the wheezle he's gat.'

wherryefer, an inquiry about one's destination: 'Hello there, Sammy. Wherryefer?'

whinge, complain, whine: 'You always know he'll start to whinge if he's not enjoyin himself.' 'He'll whinge away there if he doesn't get what he wants.'

whoosthisthonis, inquiry about a previously-encountered person: 'Whoosthisthonis? That fella with the limp. I've seen him before.' 'Her in the high heels? I know her well. Whoosthisthonis?'

willicks, variety of sea snail: 'He's a great man for gatherin willicks.' 'He says there's nathin to bate a feed of willicks.'

win, current of air: 'Ye cudden hear yer ears for the win.' 'See them tyres? What I nivver had to put in them was win.'

windy, opening in the wall of a building, usually fitted with glass: 'She even gets the windy cleaner to wash the windy of her tavishun set. Didye ivver hear the like of it?'

windy stool, window sill: 'They were sittin on the windy stool hevin a wee chat.'

wire, climate: 'The wire in this place wud drive ye astray in the head.' 'This is terrible wire. It hasn't stapt rainin for four years.'

wiresawful, extreme climatic conditions: 'This wiresawful. All we can do is go home.' 'The wiresawful. We'll just take ourselves aff.'

wise up, explain, make a set of circumstances clear to someone in ignorance of the facts: 'Ach come on. It's time for you to wise up everybody about what happened.' 'I'm sittin here waitin for you to wise me up.'

wisnae, a negative statement: 'He said he'd be there but he wisnae.' 'I told him I wisnae coming and he was all cut.' 'It was a great day for the trip. There wisnae a cloud in the sky.'

worda, male parent: 'I went for a wee walk with worda.' 'Worda bought us sweeties.'

worral, capable of, able to: 'We have a new car worral do fifty to the gallon.' 'She's a chile worral do what she's told.'

wortee, evening meal: 'We usually have a fry for wortee.' 'I'm awayon. I havta go in for wortee.'

wrap, knock: 'Please wrap before leaving milk.'

wuncenferall, indication of finality: 'I'm tellin ye wuncenferall it's my last word.' 'I tole her. Wuncenferall that's the enn of it.'

wunnathem, person of a different persuasion from the speaker: 'Watch out. He might be wunnathem.' 'How was I to know he was wunnathem?' 'If he was wunnathem why didn't he say so?'

wunnenn, stand up, rise: 'Get on yer wunnenn and we'll be on our way.' 'It's about time we were goin. Get on yer wunnenn wud ye?'

wyer, whether: 'When he put it to me I tole him I was going wyer he liked it or not.' 'How do I know wyer it's goin till rain?'

yallrite, inquiry after health or financial state: 'Yallrite again? Ye hadda bad time.' 'Yallrite ni ye've had a wee rest?' 'Yallrite? But sure ye must be, seein it's pay day.'

yap, person who is constantly complaining: 'Sure she's only an oul yap.' 'My oul woman's nathin but a natural born yap.'

yard, toilet, bathroom: 'The new house we're in is all right but it's hard gettin used to the yard bein upstairs.'

yella man, variety of candy: 'My man's like a chile. He's dyin about yella man.' 'Yella man's all right, but it's hard on the oul teeth.'

yerinfritni, a warning of danger ahead: 'Yerinfritni. Yer da's ragin mad at what ye done.' 'Yerinfritni for takin the car without astin him. Ye shudda ast.'

yer man, employer, husband, prominent politician, person whose name has been momentarily forgotten: 'Yer man was there as large as life.' 'The first fella I run intil was yer man.' 'Yer man was on the bax again last night. Every time I switch on there he is, yappin.'

yessam, an affirmation: 'Yessam goin for I promised I wud.' 'Yessam gettin up, ma.'

yilhafta, indicates necessity of a certain course of action: 'Yilhafta go or there'll be trouble.' 'Yilhafta be there on time or I'll have it in for ye.' 'Yilhafta behave yerself or we won't go.'

84

yin, one: 'Ma, we larned at school the day that yin an yin makes twa.' 'She's a funny yin, that new woman next door. She tole me her man cudden even drive a nail in a turmit.'

yo, female sheep: 'There's yin yo ahint the slap on her back an it canny get up.'

youse gettin, seeks to establish if a customer is being served: 'Youse gettin? If yer nat what can I do fer ye?' 'Youse gettin? What's yer complaint?'

yousens, you (plural): 'Tell yousens arwuns is ready to start.' 'Are youssens goin to Majorkey again for yer holidays?'

you stannin, challenge to one's generosity: 'You stannin, fer I'm nat? I'm skint.' 'You stannin? It's about time.'

yowtlin, infant: 'The wee yowtlin's cryin her head aff.'

yupyit, inquires whether the person addressed has risen from bed: 'Yupyit? The horns is blew.' 'Yupyit? Stime ye were on yer way.'

Z, uppermost part of the body: 'I tole him to play wayis Z.' 'If that wee centre wud onny play wayis Z we'd be on the pig's back.' 'It's a pity he lost his Z, sotis.'

zit, an inquiry, a question: 'Zit that time already.' 'Zit time I put on the pan?' 'Zit time we were on our way?'

zon, certain to happen: 'Zon all right, for I gat two stann tickets.' 'That cap I bought Sardy? Man dear, zon my head.'

86